THE WANDERING HEART

A Tale of a Misfit Traveling in Life's Wilderness

DANI ROSENBLAD JAMES

Introduction

Welcome to *The Wandering Heart: A Tale of a Misfit Traveling in Life's Wilderness*. This book is a journey through the landscapes of my life, interwoven with threads of adventure, struggle, resilience, and transformation. It is a story for anyone who has ever felt out of place, for those who wander in search of meaning, and for every soul yearning for connection and understanding.

My life changed in an instant as a traumatic brain injury thrust me into a world of chaos and uncertainty. The path to recovery was neither straight nor easy. It was a winding road filled with moments of profound despair and unexpected joy. There were challenges that tested my limits, and experiences that reshaped my understanding of myself and the world around me.

Nature became my refuge, my therapy, and my teacher. From the deep depths of the Amazon jungles of Peru to the workings of within, each destination offered not just a change of scenery, but a new perspective on life. These journeys, both internal and external, helped me piece together the fragments of my shattered identity and forge a new path forward.

This book is more than loosely based on my life; it is an exploration of what it means to be a misfit in a world that often demands conformity. It is about grasping onto our unique journeys, finding beauty in our struggles, and discovering strength in our vulnerabilities. Through vivid storytelling and raw honesty, I invite you to walk with me through the highs and lows, the triumphs and tribulations, and the moments of quiet revelation that have defined my journey.

As you turn these pages, my hope is that you find inspiration, comfort, and perhaps a bit of your own story reflected in mine. Whether you are navigating your own wilderness or simply seeking a deeper understanding of the human spirit, may this book remind you that even in our darkest moments, we are never truly alone. There is always a way forward, a path to healing, and a light waiting to guide us home.

Thank you for joining me on this journey. May "The Wandering Heart" resonate with your own experiences and inspire you to embrace the wild, unpredictable, and beautiful journey of life.

With gratitude,
Dani Rosenblad James
misfitwanders.com

Table of Contents

CHAPTER 1

A Smack to the Face (Present)

That foreboding feeling wasn't letting up and lingered within me as I kept driving on the black ice. Quickly, visibility became almost nonexistent since it was less than a mile. Panic boomed through me. But in that same instance, I had a realization that I needed to keep it together for my dog and for myself so that we could make it to Cali. Once I realized that, a calmness washed over me. Even with my hands feeling like they were shaking a bit, I told myself, *it's going to be okay*. That was until I saw it! The long semi-truck blocking all the lanes, and five cars piled up against it, some of them looked like a pile of tin cans. From that moment, all I remember is saying, "Oh, shit!"

That's when everything went black. My body went into autopilot and took over by veering to the right, as though I could make an invisible lane. But since I was on black ice, all I could do was slide into the heap of crumpled cars. The squealing of tires echoed in my head as I was swallowed up by the darkness and fell further into it. The deafening sound of metal being peeled off the top of my truck echoed in the air. At that same time, a long gash was left on the left side of my head. In that moment, my body turned into a rag doll being thrown back and forth from the impact and the spinning of the vehicle. Yet again, my truck hit the cars after spinning around. From that, my head was tossed to and fro, and I ended up with 4 concussions and 3 internal bleeds in my head.

Besides that, if I had been any taller the cut that I got in my head would have decapitated me. What a thought!? Blood gushed out of me slowly and steadily. Luckily, it was cold enough that my body tried to hold in as much of the essence of my life inside as it could. Right after the crash, an overwhelming pain took over my head and nothing, but the sense of darkness was there.

Ten minutes or so passed and finally, a sheriff with an exhausted face and a gray mustache came to the scene with his sirens wailing. As he gazed over the area with his weary eyes, he was overwhelmed with sadness. I looked like a crumpled-up bloody corpse. Then, he saw me move, and quickly rushed to my side jingling from the keys on his hip. I held my hand up to my head, trying to relieve the pain and I kept repeating, "My head, my head." As though that would stop the pain. He scanned me over and evaluated the situation within seconds. His piercing blue eyes took in every detail. The wrinkles in his forehead furrowed and his heart beat faster as his positivity began to falter. The small truck had turned into a convertible and the front was crushed.

Blood was splattered everywhere, it just kept coming out of my head, and now I was covered in it. My hair was plastered to my head, making it look even redder than normal from the blood. Pieces of glass were scattered everywhere, and my body was hunched over in my seat. The chill in the air held a bite to it and helped my blood have a slower flow. At this time, I was just in a darkness and everything else felt unreal.

The sheriff made an urgent call and had them send over a helicopter, which would take me to Salt Lake City, Utah. In Wyoming, they didn't have the facilities to help me with how roughed up I was. The helicopter didn't take too long to make it there and since the roads were as they were, it flew down and parked right on the icy road. Several people hopped out of it that were covered in full white gear to help me as I kept going in and out of consciousness. Once they put me inside of the helicopter, a murmur between them overtook the enclosed area. They decided abruptly to induce me into a coma and then intubate me.

Once the helicopter had left, the sheriff took an overview of the white rumpled-up tiny truck to get any clues as to who I was and where I was headed. He felt fear throughout his body and in his chest. While he evaluated the truck, he kept thinking, *how could something so horrible happen to such a young girl?* That's when he noticed the sack of dog food. Confusion overtook him and he started scanning the landscape with his eyes. Just then, he saw two black ears pop up from over a snow-covered hill. Then, popped up big yellow eyes followed by a gray spotted snout. Clyde stared at the sheriff with uncertainty.

The sheriff scratched his head as he thought about how he would be able to get this dog into his car. After grabbing the dog food and loading it into his trunk, he opened the backseat door, looked at Clyde, and said, "Load up!" It worked like magic and Clyde with a reluctant feeling got in wondering where his mom was the whole time. His eyes held all his worry, and the sheriff could sense it. The weary sheriff felt that he couldn't reassure this furball since this was the worst accident that he'd seen in his whole career, and he was going to be retiring in the next few weeks.

The news of my accident made it to my parents within hours. A burly sheriff with a heavy heart rang their doorbell in South Dakota and my father walked heavy footed over and opened the door with confusion. The sheriff started it off by saying, "I think you need to talk to a priest." With that, my father's eyes grew big and once the sheriff explained what had happened, my dad dropped to his knees and began to break down in tears. He began to wail loudly, and my mom hurriedly came over. Then she was told the news as well. But her reaction was the complete opposite of my dad's. She kept herself composed for the both of them and started asking analytical questions regarding it.

"Has her coma been induced?" She asked as she bent over to pat my dad's back.

"Well, all I know is that a helicopter picked her up and flew her to Salt Lake City, Utah." He stated.

After talking a bit more, the sheriff left with a sorrow-filled heart. Then my parents contemplated how they should get to Utah. The two quickly decided flying was out of the question since the next flight wasn't until the next day. So, driving it was. While they hastily packed, they found someone to watch their dog and made some calls to let the rest of the family know what was happening. Once they called my best friend Peggie, who was a pregnant short lady, they were told that she was coming too and that there was no way around it.

So, with a 6-month-pregnant short feisty lady in the back of their big truck and my two parents in the front, they drove as safely as they could on the rough roads. The truck was filled with a thick silence from all the worry in the air. While they drove, they ended up having to drive on the black ice in another spot of the state as well. The drive took about a day of nonstop driving with a sound-asleep Peggie in the back for half of the trip.

As exhausted as can be, my dad finally asked Peggie to drive since she was asleep most of the trip and had woken up. Her body beamed with life, and she was full of energy. So, she happily drove the rest of the way. As they drove my dad was convinced that they should see the vehicle first. But my mom vetoed that and thought it was best to get Clyde in Rock Springs, Wyoming, where the accident happened. Then head to the ICU at the Intermountain Hospital in Salt Lake City, Utah.

Howls and barks echoed within the pound as they followed the man who had taken in Clyde. He ushered them to the back that was a bit away from the other dogs. Clyde was curled up in a ball and seemed so skittish. When he looked up and saw the three of them, a feeling of relief came over him, and he began to wag his tail frantically. The three were so happy that nothing had happened to him, and they were flabbergasted that he seemed perfectly fine from being thrown from the truck. Once they got back into their truck, Clyde sat almost on top of my mom in the back, which would never have happened before. It seems that he was on high alert and didn't know what to expect when getting into a truck again.

A feeling of uneasiness crept up on my dad as they rolled up to the hospital. They had no idea how bad I was or what they would find. The three of them began walking in with Clyde close to their side. My mom did the talking since my father looked like he would burst into tears at any second. When they mentioned who they were looking for, a nurse came out quickly and knew exactly where to bring them. She immediately felt at ease that there was family here that I could be reunited with.

She quickly informed my mom as they walked. "She was induced in a coma on the helicopter and had been intubated. We found out that she had around 4 concussions and 3 internal bleeds." My mom was swept with relief about the coma. Since I was induced in a coma, it means that my head wouldn't be as damaged as if it had happened from the impact. However, the other news concerned her a bit. But she gulped down that fear for her and my dad's sake.

Once they came to the room, I was asleep with my hand resting on my head, subconsciously thinking that my hand could make a difference. Since I was induced in a coma, a feeling of being out of it lasted for about 3 days. At some point in that time, I wanted to leave, which became a yelling match between me and the nurses, where one of the nurses finally threatened to tie me down.

Anger slithered through me. My freedom was slipping through my fingers. I didn't want to be caged up in this room. My mind kept telling me that I was perfectly fine, even though I wasn't truly there in my head yet. I didn't see anything wrong with leaving, even though my balance was almost nonexistent.

Finally, Peggie with her small frame was able to get me to settle down. Her chocolate brown eyes and bouncy blonde hair relaxed me. In that moment, she put her hand on me that radiated warmth and love. Then Peggie told me that she was there and that I had Clyde. Hearing those words helped my mood improve and my anger eased. I wasn't alone. My family was here, and I wasn't going through this all by myself.

Even though I didn't understand anything about what was happening, it felt somewhat better. A brief feeling of calmness washed over me before I fell asleep again.

Since my balance had vanished, showers were a hassle, and I had to have help from two nurses. My tall thin frame was incorporative at times, making it even more difficult for the short, hefty lady and tall lanky nurse. It felt as though I was a wacky and waving inflatable tube man that just didn't give a damn. When all of this was going on, my father couldn't grasp what was happening to his *baby* girl. So, he was in panic mode. Ultimately when I would get like that, my mother would have to get her knowledge out and try to explain to him that I was healing. This would end up calming him. Since she is a retired nurse, she understood the technical terms and what happens to the body from impact much more than an average person.

While the days went by, my bestie would just stare at me and grimace from watching me try to move. I looked like a rag doll, so weak and frail to move on my own. Her heart would sink as she saw me flinch in pain yet again. Just then, she remembered that it could have been much worse. That's what finally eased her heart and helped her stay by my side.

Every day when I was still out of it, I would say, "River, River", as I cradled my head and all three of them would look at each other baffled. *What is River? Is it an actual river? Is it a person?* Somehow my phone survived the accident, and they were able to find out more about this *River*. They found out that River was the nickname of a young man that I was supposed to pick up from San Fran airport. Luckily, they found this out and were able to reach out to him. We were going to stay at my crazy fun lady friend's place who lived in Oakland. So, River called her up for a ride with a hint of sadness in his voice after he had found out the unexpected news about me.

After about three days, I finally came to fully. Relief showered over my parents once I was finally conscious, and I acted as though I was fully aware. I felt more lucid, but I still needed help with walking since my balance was still a bit off. A cloud had lifted from my head, and I didn't fully understand what had happened. So, I asked them about it with a blur in my mind. They talked to me with soothing voices as they explained how I was with the nurses and with them. From that talk, I had learned about Peggie and how she couldn't stay any longer because of her job. But she had been hesitant about going back until my mom assured her that I'd be okay.

As she told me these things, my heart had dropped. "Clyde! Where's Clyde!?" I began to panic in the bed, and I looked around frantically as I sat up. My mom gently held my hand and calmly said, "Clyde is fine." My heart softened and my adrenaline lessened when I heard that. Learning that was such a comfort. I let my body fall back down and tiredness washed over me. The energy I gave off from that action was enough to leave me exhausted.

My mom told me how at first Clyde had gotten to lay in the bed with me while my mom would read a story to me. But Clyde felt he was on guard duty and began to get too protective of me, which turned into the nurses avoiding coming in. Eventually, he was becoming too much of a hassle for the nurses and my parents put him inside their truck. Since he was in the truck, my parents would check on him throughout the day while I was still coming in and out of being coherent. A breath that I didn't notice that I was holding was let out and worry left when I learned more about Clyde. He's always been my soulmate and has always had my back while I've grown up. So, it's hard to imagine a day without him.

As I learned more about what happened, a memory came back to me in a whirlwind.

The wind howled and pushed against my small white pick-up truck. It felt like I was playing tug a war with the wind and my steering wheel. From that, it felt like the weather was on my side as I drove down the road in Wyoming. I thought today would have been better than the night before since I had stayed the night at a cheap hotel. I thought I could wait out the unpleasant feeling fizzing in my stomach from the bad weather. But that wasn't the case. I kept pushing forward and I started this journey from South Dakota. I wasn't ready to throw in the towel here. So, even with my mind racing, I drove further down the interstate.

Now, at noon, the weather wasn't any better. Thoughts whirled in my head, *they wouldn't keep the interstate open if it's too dangerous, right?*

While I drove down the interstate a foreboding feeling engulfed my body as I hit the black ice. My adrenaline started to pump faster, and my nerves were standing on end. Just then, I took a deep breath, looked at my furry soulmate, and said, "It's okay. I can do this." Clyde's fierce yellow eyes stared back at me with full trust. His curly peppered tail wagged, and he gave me a quick reassuring lick on my hand. That's just what I needed to calm down.

When I tried taking the memory and information in, my head began thumping and I quickly grabbed it, hoping that my hand would be able to stop it. But the pain came in a roar through my ears and completely engulfed my skull. My mom asked, "Do you want some pain medication?" As I held my head and laid my head back down, I responded weakly through the pain, "No".

Finally, I caved in for some Advil, which helped after a bit of time. In that instant, even though I felt like I wasn't fully there, I knew that I didn't want pain medication. Throughout the whole healing process, I repeatedly said that I didn't want any medication. Not even for how excruciating the pain was, I didn't want it. The doctor seemed to get frustrated and once threw down the notebook. He was just concerned for me, and I knew that. But I still held my ground. I wanted to feel what my body could and couldn't do. Even in this state, I knew that I needed to listen to my body and what it wanted, which was a whole lot of sleep and more rest.

While all this was happening, I could remember myself enough that if I didn't feel any pain I would overdo it and end up hurting myself in the long run. So, I endured. Plus, I didn't want to have to be stuck taking something when, for some reason, I knew that I would get better.

It was this underlying feeling within me that kept whispering to me that where I was at that moment was that, but a moment. It whispered to me, "This is but a moment." over and over. My future self wouldn't be like this and since I was missing my ego and many of my past thoughts, it was easier to listen to that inner voice.

After the pain had faded and I was able to think again, I looked at my mom with her wavy brown hair. Her eyes had dark bags under them, and she looked worn down. Then my eyes wandered to my dad who was passed out on the couch with his limbs all sprawled out. Just from his body, I could tell he was exhausted. My eyes went back to my mom, and I held her hand weakly.

"Can I see Clyde?" I asked with sadness in my eyes.

I wanted him and I felt a pang within my heart that we had to be apart. My mom's eyes softened, and she said, "First, let's see if we can get a wheelchair for you." When she said that, my eyes sparkled, and my heart filled with joy!

After some time, we were finally able to get a nurse coaxed into getting us a wheelchair and letting us venture out. My heart pounded with excitement and, surprisingly, I got into the wheelchair relatively easily. Since it took a while to get the wheelchair, my dad had woken up and my mom stated that we would visit Clyde. He could see how much that meant to me and he decided to try to sleep a little bit more since I was with my mom.

It felt like time had paused and that we would never get to the bottom floor and to the garden area. At last, we made it. Since there was an issue with Clyde being in the room, my parents had parked the truck near here so they could let Clyde out in the garden. My heart leapt as we strolled up to the truck. My mom grabbed the door handle and opened the door.

Quickly Clyde hopped out with a huge grin, and he didn't miss a beat to start running to me. I was ecstatic and held out my arms for my lovely boy. He tried sitting on my lap, but that didn't work out so well. So, he stayed on his hind legs, which put him halfway in my lap. I was filled to the brim with happiness at that moment. He was whole and I was whole. This is just what I needed. Tears streamed down my face as I held him and I kept thinking, *Thank you! Thank you!*

Over ten days of being stuck in the ICU, I had to do all kinds of tests. From that, I felt drained. My body felt heavy. It was like energy was sucked dry from me. Day in and day out, the same tests. It seemed like all of it was lasting forever. My patience was nonexistent, and I was ready to go home. So, I kept pestering them about when I would be able to go. Finally, after ten days, there was a physical exam and a mental test that I had to pass. On top of that, I would have to pass a test that I call the commonsense test.

When I did the commonsense test, I had to go into a kitchen, and a nurse would watch me diligently to make sure that I did all the things that we as humans don't focus on. These are habits that are on autopilot that many of us may take for granted. For instance, remembering to use hot pads when grabbing something hot off the stove. Or, remembering to turn off the stove after use. Once I had passed all these different tests, my doctor was still reluctant to let me go. But finally, with an unconvinced face, he signed me out. A smile crept onto my face and the feeling of freedom overtook me. It felt good not to be trapped any longer.

My mom had a discussion with the doctor quietly while my dad grabbed things and helped me along my way to the car. Now, I can walk relatively by myself. But that equilibrium of mine was not yet on my side.

So, I would sway sometimes and not completely be there. At times, it felt like my world was moving and I couldn't get my balance under me. When that would happen though, I would try to brush it off.

Once we made it to the truck with Clyde in it, relief sank in deeply. I took one long glance at the hospital before turning back to the truck. My new journey has begun. A big breath of worry left me; I was free.

CHAPTER 2

The Carefree Life (Past)

The smell of whiskey wafted to my nostrils, making me excited for what was to come. Many people seemed to be prancing around the room and dancing along with the booming music. A group cheered naked while they basked in the moonlight in the hot tub. My body tingled from being high off the environment and my judgment was quickly losing to reality. Each shot I took was leading me to autopilot where I was all about my impulses.

"Bonnie!" yelled Gina, and quickly I came back into reality with my glassy eyes. I walked over to her with curiosity in each unbalanced step. She divulged to me about this guy who she's had her eye on for years and she knew that he wouldn't be able to turn down *the pussy platter*. So, I sauntered over to him as my vision blurred in and out. I used my light touch on his arm as a weapon and brought him to Gina's room with a mischievous grin. Gina was already waiting there in her bed, and Dean had a perplexing look on his face. Then it clicked and his eyes grew wide.

Dean gawked at us with his almond brown eyes. He couldn't believe what was happening and he was so blitzed on coke that no matter how much we tried, he just couldn't get it up. Gina's heart dropped when she realized that he was useless right now. The two of us left the room unsatisfied and decided to take on new indulgences at the party.

The night went on with us running around half-naked with others. We would enjoy the hot tub for a bit and then abruptly get out to do something else. Nobody could sit still. The atmosphere held its own drug while people scampered around. It wasn't until around six in the morning that the crowd on the porch finally died down. My body couldn't handle alcohol anymore. So, I finally passed out next to a topless Gina with Dean in her tattered bed.

The next morning, I woke up with a pounding in my head. My phone was cast aside at some point among the scattered clothes on the floor and I finally started to move around to start my day. My Australian cattle dog with his curly tail lay at my feet. He had black fur patches over both eyes and his penetrating yellow eyes rang out how intelligent he was. I began to scurry around as he rested his head on the bed. During this time, I could feel what he was thinking as his stare burned my skin. Another night of debauchery out in the boonies of North California. The land was known for its pot plants and as the area that was in the gray zone with the law. My head thrummed with each step I took as I gathered my things, got dressed, and headed out.

It was time for Clyde and me to get back to the

property. There was a lot of work to do, and I didn't have any time to dawdle. Finally, we reached our hidden-away spot up on a mountain that's out of the hands of reception. Since it's about 15 minutes from town, it has a whole other feel to it. The day started off in a daze and once I finally started to sober, it was time to work in the sun's rays while it pelted down on my exhausted body. Yet another party in between the blazing sun with the long days working out in the heat. But somehow this soothed me. Even though my head was hammering away, being out in nature opened something within me.

The field of scattered marijuana plants that I worked in was enclosed by tall trees, giving it a feeling of being secluded. When I got into the tiny cabin with a rundown oven and a camper stove next to it, I quickly changed my clothes into my permeated working clothes, a pistol strapped to my hip and weed clippers in another pocket. Since I was healing from the night before, I decided that I would work with the plants barehanded. So, my gloves went into my back pocket, and off we went to the top on the four-wheeler.

Once the engine roared to life, Clyde jumped up for joy. He knew this meant he would get to run in front of the quad to the top, which he loved to do! I sped to the top with Clyde leading the way and cheerfully barking every now and again. The breeze calmed me as the wind cooled my pounding head. Each turn relaxed me since I was fully submerged in the wilderness. I was starting to feel better. As we made it to the top, I took in a deep breath with my eyes closed and let it out. *How lucky was I to be up here within nature and be able to work every day with my dog by my side?* I thought.

In the distance, you could see the pine trees dance in the breeze on the neighboring mountaintop. My heart thrummed with happiness as I started working away on the plants. I touched the leaves, and a prickly feeling crept through my hands. Along with that, my insides started to warm up giving me a small high as I plucked away some of the leaves. My head started to clear, and my whole body began to relax more. A sigh released from my lips, and I was in bliss.

Since I had trouble listening to audiobooks while I worked, I would listen to music. This gave me a lot of time to self-reflect or ponder on little thoughts here and there. My mind began to replay the night before. A giggle came out of me as I shook my head. *Oh, Bonnie!* I thought to myself.

After that, I had time to contemplate what I was doing as a person. First off, I was kind of a shit person. This was true when it came to guys. I just saw them as something to fuck and nothing else. I mean, I had many guy friends. But relationships were definitely not my strong suit. A feeling of disgust grew within me. It burrowed far within my gut and felt like it was starting to fester. *Why was I this way?* At that moment, I realized that I didn't want to be that kind of person any longer. As the thought came out, I decided right then I wouldn't be that way any longer.

But just as I thought about that, my hunger rose. My veins felt like they were on fire and just the thought of sex ignited me. I tried to avoid those kinds of thoughts. But they came flooding in with Gina and my escapades on finding our victims. This appetite of mine was something that I had trouble satisfying and I had no urge to deal with it. But it felt almost as important as it does to eat. *What a problem!*

Because of that hunger, being on the mountain alone can be tough. Especially when you have this kind of craving that feels as though it's eating you away. My body wouldn't calm down. So, it meant that night would be yet another party night with my girlfriend Gina. The long hot day took my attention away from that burning desire to a point. But after taking a shower and cooling down, it came back with vengeance. My mind couldn't think of anything else. It was as though my mind was plagued with dirty thoughts that kept persisting. So, I quickly got dressed in a cotton-red dress and headed out with Clyde by my side.

I rolled up to the coffee shop, which was one of the places to go to for nighttime fun in the tiny town of around 2,000 people. The dirt parking lot had a nice shady spot. So, Clyde stayed in the truck outside. I walked up the steps with a hop of excitement. The wooden building looked cozy and welcoming from the outside and one of Gina's creative chalk art creations of a fat guy chugging a beer was on the sign. Once I was inside, I scanned the room, taking in the old wooden piano and the long wooden bar along with several tables scattered throughout half of the room. They had their stage prepared with speakers, microphones and it seemed that it was soon time for a band. These kinds of nights can get rough and rowdy, which excites me!

A grin sprawled over my face. Then, I saw Gina with her short brown hair behind the counter shuffling through the glasses. She turned around when she saw me and poured out an IPA for me in a glass. She was grinning from ear to ear. Her eye had been on this guy across the room, and she already could sense why I came in. I followed her gaze that had a glint of mischief and saw Sam, a tall broad-shouldered guy with brown wavy shoulder-length hair. This guy definitely had one of those mouths that made you either love him or hate him.

The first time that I had met him, I couldn't tell whether I wanted to kiss him or put a sock in his mouth. But I did know that I had some kind of pull to him that I couldn't explain. It was like I kept feeling some kind of electric wave pulling us closer. Just being around him would make me wet and when his gaze lingered on me, I could feel my mouth watering. So, I strolled over there, gave him a big hug, and found out what his plan was for the night. Once he told me that he had no plans, my mind went to work on how the night would play out and I felt an electric feeling come to life inside of me.

After many drinks and staying until Gina closed, the three of us left together with my dog at our heels. This was another night of the pussy platter, and I was fully satiated. When I was able to take care of that hunger, I could calm down. In the moments when this feeling would overtake me, thinking became a chore to do. It made me feel as though I wasn't human. This feeling has gotten me into a lot of weird situations and a lot of sex with people that I wouldn't have otherwise if they were elsewhere when my need for sex erupted. But the sex craving is what bonded Gina and I so quickly. It seems that both of us have a high sex drive, which is great when we serve the pussy platter.

Another day passed on the farm and while I was on the top of the mountainside, one of our sensors went off. I stood up on high alert and put my left hand on my gun. My eyes scanned our surroundings and Clyde's ears were fully erect, listening to every sound. Immediately, I hopped on the four-wheeler and checked the front gate with Clyde sprinting in front of me. We got there and I saw our neighbor's dog sniffing our sensor. His brown-black coat had some dreads in it and his frame hunkered down since he was a bit older. A wave of relief passed over me, and I stopped a few feet from where the dog was as he scampered to the other side of the stream. There, I saw our neighbor hollering at her dog with a scrunched-up face.

When she saw me, her face turned into a cheery smile that was so welcoming. Her whole attitude completely changed as I got off the four-wheeler and walked toward this burly 40-year-old lady. The closer I got, the more wrinkles I could see on her and every time I saw her, she had a piece of straw hanging from her mouth. The atmosphere around her felt like she was someone who you didn't want to piss off. So, it was great that she took a liking to me, which I think was due to me having a gun on my hip and not being afraid of getting dirty. She knew that I was a hard worker and that was something that she respected. Plus, meeting a young girl like me working on the mountain made her beam with joy. Especially, since she had the chance to randomly talk to me down by the stream.

"How's it goin'?!" She yelled as I headed her way. My shorts were covered in resin and my tank looked like it had seen better days since it had a couple of holes and dirt spots all over.

"Oh, you know, working away! And yourself?" I called back. Now, I was next to the stream with Clyde by my side. But once we started talking, Clyde walked in the clear water to sniff the other dog. The both of them wagged their tails uncontrollably as they sniffed one another. I watched them in my peripherals as I talked with the neighbor, making sure that they got along. An inner worry lifted, and I came back to reality with the neighbor asking me if I knew what happened on her property last year. "I don't think so. What happened?" Her eyes filled with excitement, and she began to tell me the story of the stupid guy who came onto her property.

It was around dawn and the neighbor was doing her daily walks on the property. Then she saw him! A scruffy skinny guy in overalls with a few holes in the pant legs. He was snipping off the buds from her plants and quickly stuffed them into his pockets. With a loud bellow, the neighbor shouted, "What the hell are you doing on my property again!?" The guy froze in place and held up his hands. "I told you the next time you come har, I was goin' take something from ya!" With that being said, she pulled her trigger and let the shot ring out. She took off the guy's right hand and his scream filled the hillside. He scurried away holding onto his bleeding stub.

The neighbor laughed as she finished her story, and I stared back at her in bewilderment. I didn't know what to think. "After that, that dummy was seen in town and now he'd bin known as a weed thief! It's hard not to spot a guy missing his hand! And it was freshly taken too!" She chuckled. My eyes grew wide as she told her story.

Sometimes I forget that this is my reality…

CHAPTER 3

Recover in the Midwest (Present)

It was like I was coming out of a fog. I opened my eyes and waited for them to adjust. My world was moving in and out. Then I started to remember that I was in the truck with my parents and Clyde. Suddenly, it hit me. I had been in the hospital, and now we're in the truck on our way back to South Dakota. Pain smashed into me once again, and I held my head as I sat up. It slowly subsided as I let my panic thoughts go. My mom turned back to me and said, "Good, you're up." With a happy tone in her voice that somehow annoyed me since I was in pain. But I get it. She's happy that I'm alive and in one piece.

My dad, on the other hand, was filled with worry since I'd been sleeping most of the trip. Before I dozed off the first time, I remember that I had this feeling like I was being pulled down. But I could hear everything and there was a frantic pitch to my dad's tone as he asked my mom why I was sleeping so much. Then he quickly asked if I was okay. So, my mom, being the lady that she is, reassured him that this is a way to heal. My body needed the extra rest to heal, and it is not something that you could easily fix. That was the last I heard before I faded into the darkness once again.

A peaceful feeling overflowed as I thought about

sleep. Just then, we hit a bump, and my body thrummed with pain. No wonder my body wanted to sleep so much. This ride was hard. After a few hours, we finally made it to a hotel for the night and the only thought I had was, finally. A sigh of relief came out of me as each cell in my body ached as if I'd been doing some intense activity that used the whole body.

We got a room, and I could feel that I needed a shower, badly! Once we got settled in our room, all I could think about was washing this broken feeling off. *If only it was that easy.* I could imagine washing off my inner pain and giving my mind some way out of this struggle. But it was difficult for me to keep my focus on that because of the oncoming pain.

I gazed at my parents and saw that they were exhausted as well. As I stared at my mom, I said, "I'm going to shower." I thought she was going to fight me on it since I had nurses help me before. But she just nodded her head as she and my dad proceeded to watch TV. *Huh, that was easy*, I thought. After getting undressed and into the shower, the water pounding down on my body felt good and hurt a little bit from my body being so sensitive as well.

Suddenly, my world started spinning and I felt like I was going to hit the floor. But I reached my hand out just in time to grab the handle inside the shower. My heart was racing, and I didn't understand what had happened. One minute I was just standing there and then the next, I almost face-planted it in the tub. After waiting for my nerves to calm down, I ended up sitting in the shower and finished cleaning while I had my legs crossed. *I'm an independent grown-ass woman. I don't need my mom to help me shower,* I thought. My stubbornness started to peak its head out and a wave of anger came with it. *I'm not going to let my freedom be taken away.* I thought as I finished showering, got dressed and brushed my teeth.

We only stayed a night there and the next day we got back on the highway. The road to my parents' home finally came into view and happiness overflowed within me. The first thought that popped in was, *I can lay down.* What a weird thought since that's what I'd been doing most of the ride. I kept thinking, *Wouldn't I want to stretch my legs and maybe go on a walk?* But I guess that wouldn't work out so well since my legs felt wobbly and my balance was crap.

My body felt worn out as though it was a ragged cloth covered in holes. I dragged my feet inside my parents' house and went up to the room that I had used when I visited them. My body became heavier, and I knew that I needed to rest. Clyde stayed right at my toes and never left my side. He could sense how much pain I was in and as I looked at him while I lay in bed, I gave him a weak smile as I petted him. His tail started to whip back and forth, and it looked as if he smiled back. A darkness consumed my eyesight again, and I was asleep.

As I rested with Clyde by my side in the guest room, my parents made many calls to family and friends to let them know what was happening. At this moment, I kept going in and out of sleep. It was hard for me to keep focus and the thoughts in my head became erratic. I closed my eyes and took a deep breath and then I let it all go. I let myself just be.

While I was in this state, I opened up to myself and found that I was empty. It felt like I was missing a huge part of what made me, well, ME. The feeling of being lost rushed over me and I had no idea how to get that missing part back. Worry ensued as I wandered the darkness in my mind. No echo could be heard in here, and nothing could be seen. However, I felt comfortable in this emptiness. My hand in front of my face was practically invisible. Then reality came back once my parents called my name and just as quickly, I lost that dark place that I felt so comfortable in.

After talking with my parents for a bit while I lay in bed, sleep tugged at me. My parents headed back downstairs and as soon as they left the room, I was passed out yet again. Once I woke up, I couldn't place where I was. But then a realization came to me. My thoughts started to race as I thought that I might be stuck in South Dakota once more! My heart sank as this black hole of a place grabbed me for another round. When this thought crossed my mind, a searing pain came with it. At that moment, I grabbed my head and tried to ease the pain. I let go of my thoughts and tried to think of nothing, especially NOT the pain.

Soon, it started to subside, and my thoughts started working away again. The whole reason I enjoyed working in California was that I was away from this vacuum of a place, which seemed to always suck me back in. I took a deep breath in and tried to relax. Suddenly, I felt a furry face come to my hand and force me to pet him, which helped with my anxiety and the pains in my head. He wagged his tail profusely while he had his head resting on my lap. His big eyes stared up at me with a knowing of what I needed right then.

After having the moment with Clyde, I felt it was time to leave the bed. My world spun a bit when I got up. But I was able to get on my feet and stumble down the stairs safely to my parents. My dad looked at my mom and then back at me, "You have a lawyer now for the accident..." He stated. He started to explain it in more detail and much of what he said faded out of my memory. I knew that my parents both were talking now, but it felt like I was in the air flying around. It was hard for me to grasp what they were saying, especially since I didn't feel like I was fully there. I tried coming back. However, no matter how hard I tried, the words that they said just kept tumbling out of my head, which frustrated me. I couldn't comprehend what was happening.

My mom studied my face and with sadness in her eyes, she asked if I was alright. I must have looked lost and that's exactly how I felt. But I didn't want them to know that I was completely lost in the conversation. So, I quickly nodded my head and from that action, an agonizing pain overwhelmed my head again. By reflex, I clutched my head and sat down immediately on the couch that was next to me.

After a while and after drinking some much-needed water, I looked over the documents that pertained to the lawyer. This must have been what they were talking about earlier. As I read it, I chuckled. *Why on earth would it matter if I sign this when it's obvious that I'm not fully in my head?* But I signed it anyway since I wanted to make this problem go away as soon as possible.

Later that day, I was up in my parents' room watching their TV on their bed when Jenivive came in. Her long straight blonde hair swayed with each step. My 13-year-old niece stared at me in excitement with her big pale-blue eyes. Then her look turned into confusion and her mouth dropped. All of a sudden, she began laughing. I looked at her quizzically, not understanding what was funny and then she pointed to what I was doing. Her innocent eyes held a glint of laughter as she giggled at me.

In my left hand, I had an applesauce jar, and in my other, a fork. It didn't click to me that this wasn't a good match. I mean, my go-to utensil has always been a fork. So, I thought that a fork was a logical utensil and when I told her this, she just giggled at me even more. That ended up making me grumpy since I didn't see it as wrong. Gabriella, her sister came up and when she took in what I had in my hands, she started giggling as well. Even though Gabriella is older, she's actually shorter than her younger sister, Jenivive. However, she makes up for it by being a spunky tiny thing. Both the girls have the same kind of big blue eyes and long blonde hair that lets you know that they're sisters.

They sat on the bed with me for a little bit while I watched a show. But I think both realized that I wasn't fully there and while they stared at me, I winced in pain a couple of times. Jenivive's eyes grew bigger as she saw how hurt I was. She couldn't take it anymore and whispered to Gabriella. Then they both nodded their heads to one another and said their goodbyes to me.

Once they got downstairs, they started talking to my mom quietly. I couldn't focus on what they were saying since I was in the room upstairs. It just sounded like a buzzing to me. As the pictures played on the screen in front of me, I couldn't keep focus, and I kept zoning out to nothingness.

My world became wider and nonexistent all at the same time. I was back in that dark place where nothing could be seen or heard. Yet this is where I felt the most comfortable, and even my pain would go away when I stayed here. My reality was pain. Although within me, I could find solace. A place where I felt free from being hurt and from being broken. Here, I could just be and that's all I needed.

One more day had turned into a blur and like the other days, Clyde was always by my side. I could tell that he was worried about me since he acted like he was on guard duty at all times. My body felt heavy and my head woozy. However, I forced myself to move around. I didn't want to be stuck in bed all day if I could help it. I began moving slowly but steadily as if I were a turtle and suddenly my phone started pinging from texts. Many of the messages came from friends in the area who had heard that I was back in town from my mom's post on Facebook.

One of my besties, Peggie messaged me, and a sigh of relief came from me. She would understand me more than the others. She had seen just how bad I was. *Now, if only I could get my vision to focus.* I thought as I held up the phone. It was like my vision kept blurring in and out. Every button moved out of my grasp. I started to feel frustrated with my patience. Then, I took a breath and pressed send.

A pain seared through my neck. Since I was looking down at the screen, my neck wasn't happy. It felt like a burn ignited right where I had the fracture. So, I stretched it up and then rested my head back on the couch. Everything was so exhausting, and it was hard to keep any energy within me. But I kept feeling that I had to push myself. Otherwise, I would turn into a blob on a bed. A whirlwind of feelings enraptured me. But I couldn't place them or what was happening. So, I shrugged it off and began getting ready for Peggie to pick me up after I rested my head a little. My 10-minute rest on the couch helped rejuvenate me and I got up and started walking back to my room.

After a little hop, I had my tight jeans on with my Misfit Wanders t-shirt on because what better way to promote my travel blog than to wear my logo? Since I recently came back from a trip to Peru and Bolivia, my body was in great shape. Those swirling feelings that I felt earlier from being around old friends came back as I hung out with Peggie and some of our other friends. I felt giddy out of the blue and then it sunk down and quickly turned into that lost feeling that I was getting to know so well. It was hard to be fully aware of my surroundings and I couldn't place where all these random feelings were coming from.

As our friends talked, I had trouble keeping focus on the conversations, and when it came time for me to respond, I would stumble on my words. At that moment, I could see the words in my mind, but I just couldn't get them out of my mouth. My mouth had become my enemy. It seemed like it didn't want to work with what I was thinking a lot of the time. Or, at times, it worked too well where I didn't have a filter. There was no middle ground anymore and I felt stupid that I couldn't grasp things that were normally so easy for me.

There was a nothingness between the outer world

and me. I didn't understand what was going on with me. When the words kept escaping me, this would fill me with an inner rage. *Why can't I say what I want?!* Peggie stared at me in worry. She could see that my eyes were immersed in anger and that I was frustrated with myself. Her tiny brown hand lightly patted me on my hand, which helped me focus on reality once again and my anger subsided. I was grateful. She knew me.

A few more days passed in blurs and my buddy Teddy wanted to meet up. When I got my message from him, I was thrilled since he's like my 6-foot walking teddy bear! I relied on him many times when I was a teenager, and he would usually be able to get me out of trouble since I was a spitfire. I tended to find trouble at parties, and he'd be the one bailing me out or would drive me to a safe place to crash.

When he came to pick me up from my parents, I jumped up and down. Once he got out of his car, I ran over to him and gave him a warm hug! I started asking him a bunch of questions with excitement as if I was that 16-year-old schoolgirl again. Teddy's scruffy facial hair matched his curly brown hair and when he laughed it would fill a room. This time he just chuckled at me with all the energy I seemed to have.

It wasn't until we met up with some other friends that he looked at me in worry. One of our buddies told a joke and everyone laughed, except me. It just didn't click, and I stared at them with a blank face, not sure what they wanted from me. This made many of our friends feel a bit uncomfortable. But Teddy waved it off and kept the conversation going, which helped lighten the mood. Time was starting to weigh on me. Being around a group of people felt like it had a hold on me, and I could only handle so much. I was beginning to get overstimulated with all the people, the sounds and the atmosphere.

My focus was at its limit, and I kept dazing out. I couldn't hold onto reality anymore and drifted back into my darkness. A soothing feeling washed over me, and I felt safe. It felt like my ego, personality, and beliefs were gone. So, *where was I? Isn't that what makes me, me?* My body was not my own and I couldn't recognize it anymore as I floated in the darkness.

Abruptly, Teddy got me back into reality. "Are you alright?" He asked with a concerned look on his face. I smiled at him still with that feeling of calmness, "Of course."

Many of my days had turned into being busy with doctor appointments. This involved physical therapy, mental tests, and many other kinds of tests. Once my mom brought me to the rehabilitation center, I was immersed in pain. It was like all the people's thoughts and feelings combined within me and engulfed me in chaos. I could hear nothing and everything at the same time. When this happened, I tried to slow down my nerves. But it felt like I was trying to tame a lion. All the different sounds, lights, and feelings were becoming like sharp points, stabbing me over and over.

So, as my mom filled out the papers for me, I held my head and worked on not thinking. Finally, we were called, and we met the doctor whom I told prior that I didn't want any medicine, only physical therapy. I remember when I told him this, he looked at me with a skeptical stare. However, he wrote it down and followed what I had asked. As usual, he asked me how my day-to-day was going. I just thought, *it's a day*. But I would say, "Good. I think I'm doing better."

Then, he would look at my mom and she would explain in more detail how my days were going, which is about the time that I would begin to space out. I felt like I would just zoom out of the situation and then it was almost as if I had reverted into a kid. The adults talked in front of me and in the language I knew. Yet, I couldn't understand them.

The walls felt like they were alive, and I couldn't keep my mind on one thought or really anything. The world felt real yet surreal and grasping on to what was my reality was becoming hard. I felt lost but found at the same time and my life felt chaotic yet calm. I couldn't understand any of this and it made me feel like I was going crazy. My world was spinning right in front of me, and it left me feeling uncertain.

I needed a break from all the doctor visits and, somehow, I ended up at a guy's house with my friend,

Peggie. I had never met this young man before. But something clicked within me. I was drawn to him, even though he was a bit of an ass. His lanky body with his curly brown hair reminded me of the guys that I went for in high school. My mind was ensnared by sexual desires, and I started craving him. Although he had a lady. However, that didn't seem to bother him or me. So, we met up several times and acted like rabbits.

It seems that I had turned back into how I was in my teenage years. Plus, my sex craving came back in full force, meaning that feeling of need would take over. I couldn't shake it without getting my fix. Sex had turned back into a drug for me, and I wasn't sure what my feelings were in this predicament. Besides dealing with that, I kept feeling lost and I still didn't fully understand what was happening to me. My body was acting on its own and my mind was on vacation.

Zack was a bit full of himself, but he had a fragile ego. When I told him that I just wanted sex, I could see his heart break. I looked into his eyes, and I felt nothing besides that urge for sex. I mean, he's nice to look at. But his attitude needed some work. Plus, it was easy for him to cheat on his lady. That's not someone that I would want as a boyfriend, that's for sure. This fling lasted for a month while I was back in Sioux Falls as I was healing. So, I wasn't fully back to normal. My mind and body were acting free as though I was the teenage version of myself. *Maybe that's why I was attracted to him.*

As I recovered, I had to see a mental therapist and from the tests that they gave, we learned that I had a high IQ, which surprised me. From that, we also learned that my attention span was limited, meaning that I had ADHD. After all those tests while I was in the car with my mom talking away, my gaze wandered to a cow in the distance. When I blinked and looked in another spot, a silhouette figure of that same cow was still in my vision. It was like the shadow of the cow had moved on its own. This started to happen frequently, and I was getting worried. Once a few days passed, I scheduled an appointment with an eye doctor.

The day came for the appointment with the eye doctor and for more tests. These tests were where I had to follow a light and press the place where it was before it went out. My patience was at an end, and I got bored quickly since I had to wait for the light or image to move for these tests. After 10 excruciating minutes, we learned that I had ADHD. Besides that, the doctor told me that I probably had it before the accident. It's just that after the accident, it had been reawakened in overdrive. Now, I would have to learn how to subdue this beast once again. Along with this information, the doctor explained that the silhouette forms were a way that my body was working through healing and that over time, it would get better. *Phew!*

Afterwards I was back at home with all the time in the world. I felt a pent-up feeling and needed to let it out. So, I decided to try to do some yoga. But as I tried to do downward dog, an excruciating pain imprisoned my head, leaving me in tears and on my side lying on the floor. My whole world felt like it tumbled down on me, and trying to think was not happening. All I could do was wish for the pain to go away... Yet another day when I had the realization that I'm not like I used to be. The pain twirled and succumbed to my whole body, leaving me crumpled up on the ground. All I could do was not move and focus on breathing.

Another issue I ran into as I hung out with my friends and Peggie was that I became annoyingly loud. As many of my friends had noticed, it was as though I was a 16-year-old again. Plus, I didn't have a sensor anymore. So, I would say whatever crossed my mind. The immature teenage version of me was alive once again. It was becoming obvious that this accident had reversed me back in time. This was nonetheless something else that felt out of my grasp. I didn't understand it or how to fix it. *What can you do when you don't understand, and your brain feels like it's working against you?*

Finally, the day came where I passed all the tests. Excitement was brewing within me. I was ready to head back to Northern Cali and get back on the mountain. My friend Kay, who lives up there, would have it no other way than to come get me since she is my soulmate. The first time we had met, we just clicked, and we knew from that moment that we would be friends for life. We would do whatever we could for one another, no matter what.

I heard a rumbling outside and my eyes lit up. I knew that Kay was coming to get me in her tiny pickup. So, once I saw her, my heart filled with joy. Kay bounced out of her truck and walked straight towards me with a skip in her step. Her light wavy brown hair moved back and forth with every step. As I crept closer to her, I could see in her eyes that she was filled with concern mixed with happiness. But that didn't matter, and we held each other in a long embrace. Until I finally introduced her to my parents. Quickly after that, I grabbed my things, Clyde, and we started to head out.

As we drove to the West Coast, my body could feel every bump and turn. It started out as a dull ache, which slowly turned into stabbing pains. I couldn't be in the car for more than a few hours without having those intense pains throughout my body. However, we made it at least halfway and from there, we drove the rest after a night of sleeping in a hotel. While Kay drove the next day, I kept going in and out of the dark place that was within me, and I think this was beginning to worry her.

Our drive didn't have a lot of conversations since I slept a lot. When I was awake, my brain was having trouble thinking of the words. But as I swayed in and out of my darkness, it felt like I didn't care how I seemed. Nothing mattered and it wasn't as though I gave up. It was the complete opposite. I found that things JUST are and there was nothing that I could do to change that. I had accepted that.

Once we made it to Cali, I felt haggard. Even as I felt that way, I kept telling myself, *everything will be alright.* Eventually, I could feel the weight in the air as Kay was beginning to realize just how damaged I was from the accident.

CHAPTER 4

The Life as a Weed Farmer (Past)

The sun pelted down as I wiped the sweat off my brow. It was another long day in the field; just me and Clyde with my gun on my hip. Dirt was smeared on my face from rolling around on the ground looking for the water leak in the hose. My shredded jeans and grey tank top were drenched in water. But it felt good with the sun's rays on my body. The day felt peaceful while I worked on de-leafing the plants which gives more life to the rest of it. Many people have told me that talking nicely and being caring towards a plant can also help with its growth. Plus, certain music with their frequencies has been shown to help. This wasn't something on my mind though as I busily took off the excess leaves. The buzzing feeling coursed through my body as I touched each leaf, and they eased any pains from the night before. I took in a deep breath of fresh air. This is what I like, being fully engulfed in nature and for some reason, I feel a connection with these marijuana plants.

Most of the time while I worked on the weed plants, I had the silence as my friend and then sometimes I would listen to music. But as hard as I tried, my mind couldn't focus on an audiobook. Boy, have I tried! So, music and my thoughts were my way of working. A breeze picked up and swirled some of the leaves in the air. They put on a little dance and then the wind stopped. Clyde's ears perked up as we heard a bark in the distance.

That's when a gnawing feeling came back into my head once again. I couldn't shake it. The stories that I had recently learned about the property weren't pleasant and the only thought that came to mind was, "*Toto, we're not in Kansas anymore!*" However, these stories were horrifying especially compared to The Wizard of Oz.

About 3 years before I started working on this property, it had been robbed! It was one of the regular hot days when this happened and there were many trimmers working away on the property. The security wasn't as strict back then, and the owner hadn't installed a fireproof metal gate yet for the driveway. So, the three guys with itchy hands were able to come in easily. Once they rolled up, one of the slender guys took out a flame torch from the black rusty van while the others grabbed a bat and a rebar. The trimmers were working away under an open tent a little bit in the distance. These men with their suspicious eyes came inside the tent immediately with their agenda.

The last one looked around the area frantically while the first guy had the confidence to start the harassing since he had the flame torch. First, he strolled up to one of the girls with big eyes and held her blonde dreads in his hand and with the other hand he held the flame torch. He kept the rusty yet still hot flame torch near her face as he screeched, "You better give us all the weed, or we might have a barbecue!" Many of the trimmers panicked and they all stopped what they were doing.

Then two of the shaky trimmers quickly started grabbing all the weed and stuffed them into the bags. It was a mix of trimmed and untrimmed marijuana. All the other trimmers looked frozen, and some had paled. The dread-haired girl had tears streaming down her face and her eyes looked lost in a far-away place. One of the trimmers with shaky hands handed the bag to the second guy who came to rob them. That man laughed at how scared the trimmers had become and he acted as though this was all a game.

After that, the first thief tossed the girl away. He was done with her. Then, the twitchy men vanished in the dust as they spun their tires and sped away. They took about 2–3 bags and left the trimmers in a tear-filled daze. Since they left so quickly, the other workers didn't even know what had happened until afterwards. So, the trimmers were left in panic and bewilderment. Some were in shock and could barely think. While others were crying profusely.

The next year after that, another accident happened on this same farm by the same three thieves. This time they showed up in full body armor with a bigger van and they were all strapped with guns. But this time the owner (my boss) had installed the fireproof metal gate and made the security a lot stricter with sensors. Besides that, the workers had walkie-talkies on their hips along with their own guns. Once the thieves drove up, a worker called the sheriff. This town was tiny, and it only had two sheriffs. So, it was lucky that one was able to make it, and this event quickly turned into a stand-off.

The sheriff with his hefty body had his hand on his gun as he talked to the three shifty men. He was finally able to talk them into leaving as one of the thieves was freaking out. The first guy who had the flame torch the year before sneered at the sheriff before they left. The panic lessened in the air as they finally drove away. Later on, we found out that the third guy who panicked at the gate ended up getting shot by the first guy. It seems that he gave the wrong intel on the property which pissed off the first man. So, he decided that he would end him, which he did.

I took a deep breath and came back to reality. *There's nothing that I can do about the past. This year will be different,* I thought as I brushed off the past stories. One of the thieves is gone and I don't think they would be stupid enough to try this place a third time. So, I tried focusing on the good with this thought. There was no need to let this get to me. I need to live in the present and focus on what I'm doing now. When that thought trailed into my head, a calming feeling overtook me and I was able to get back into the groove of working on the plants. The rest of the day went smoothly out in the sun with Clyde wandering around and sniffing the air in the area on guard duty.

The next day began, and I was awakened by the alarm buzzing to life. My eyes felt like they were filled with sand. I clicked off the alarm on my phone and then did a big stretch while I lay in bed with Clyde at my feet. When he heard me make a sound, he excitedly hopped to my face to give me morning kisses. I wrapped my arms around him in a warm cuddle that filled my heart with love. *Okay, now it's time to start the day.*

Every day has turned into a routine where I either hike up or ride the four-wheeler up the hill to the mountainside. This is where the fields of marijuana plants are, enclosed by forests. Since we have it all fenced, it helps us avoid running into hungry deer or other wild animals. However, those gophers are my arch-nemesis! They scurry underground and create huge teething marks on the roots. Sometimes the plants even die if I can't stop the gophers in time.

Once we ventured out from the cabin, Clyde did a happy jump in the air with a matching bark. As I stepped outside, I took a deep breath and relished being out in nature. A peaceful feeling burrowed within me and the two of us started our journey up the hill with my gun strapped to my side. Day in and day out, it was just me, Clyde, and the plants. During this time, I would be disconnected from the outer world since there was no reception on the property. So, no internet, and no phone calls. All that we had was a landline inside the cabin for emergencies. While I worked away on the property, Clyde was on guard duty and took that job very seriously.

Much of the day passed and I didn't feel like listening to music. So, it was the serene sounds of nature. The leaves swayed in the wind and sometimes I could hear a bird chirping. I went to each plant and made sure the drippers were working correctly as my mind wandered. I started thinking of the person who I wanted to be. No more leading guys on, no more treating them like dirt. I would see them as my equals. A smile played on my face as I accepted this new me and I began working away immersed in one of the plants.

Every time that I went up the hill or to the greenhouse, a harmonious feeling coursed through me, and it felt like I was where I was meant to be at that moment. I felt complete. My body felt like it could connect with me a lot easier when I was surrounded by the outdoors. Plus, I felt a pull to these plants, as though they were calling me to them. There were no worries or stress in my body while I was here. It felt like time stood still, and even when the heat was scorching hot, it didn't bother me. I felt whole as I worked in this magical place that was encircled by nature.

But no matter how much I enjoyed this work, I was starting to need human contact badly. There was only so much I could do with myself, and that sexual desire within me just kept growing. It was as if someone could read my mind; I got a call when I made it back to the cabin. It was Kay, my bestie soulmate! She knew me all too well and told me that she was bringing me some presents soon since it was almost harvest season. The smile in her words could be felt and I started to get excited.

My insides twirled with anticipation. I spent five months on a mountain with just Clyde and just a few times in town to interact with people. So, my people skills were at an all-time low. When the time came for my presents, panic ensnared me, and I didn't know how to act. This was the first time anyone had ever been over to this place. On other days, I stayed at my lady friends from town a couple of times. But most of my time was up on this mountainside.

The alarm at the gate dinged to life and my heart began hammering. This meant that they had made it and from what Kay had said, these guys were scrumptious to look at. *Now, I have to get my boss bitch side on and let them know who's running this place.* I thought as I put the gun on my hip and grabbed the four-wheeler key. But I wasn't used to having underlings… I felt a hesitation. Clyde's bark rang in my ears and brought me back. *That's right, I got this!*

Clyde was scurrying quickly ahead of the four-wheeler in a barking frenzy. Once I got to the gate, I jumped off the quad and took out the key from my pocket. As I was working on unlocking the gate, I couldn't see the two guys clearly. Both were in the back of the truck, and Kay stared at me with a twinkle in her eye and a grin on her face. Finally, I opened it up and Kay drove them through smoothly. Then, I locked the gate again. My heart was still pounding from the anticipation. However, this didn't affect Clyde in the least. He happily sped past me and led the way back to the cabin.

Once Clyde and I made it to the cabin, the boys got out of Kay's small truck with all their gear. When I looked over their gear, I saw that they had a tent. Then, I started to scan them over with lustful eyes. My nerves felt erratic since I couldn't calm my thoughts. Then, I hesitantly introduced myself as they brought their stuff inside. They were both smiling as they introduced themselves while they busily worked on grabbing their gear and the tent.

Bjorn, the older brother, stepped outside and started looking for a spot on the side of the mountain, which hugged the cabin. He looked for the best place with his nimble skinny tall frame and found where he wanted to set up camp. The spot that he decided on was just outside from the porch and the ground was at an angle. But that didn't stop the two from turning that area into their flat spot. Bjorn started hacking away at the side of the mountain with a pickaxe. While I watched him, I was shocked that this was no big deal for him. Then, my gaze wandered to the other brother, Carl, as he took off his shirt. I was mesmerized by his square muscular build. He grabbed a shovel without saying anything and began working alongside his brother. These two worked in silence. Heat consumed my body. My loins were burning up and I needed a break from the show.

So, I wandered back inside the cabin to meet up with Kay. She was grinning from ear to ear and a squeal came out of her as she skipped over to me. We hugged each other and it had felt like it had been forever since we had been near one another. My heart filled with such love that a serene feeling came along with happiness. We hadn't seen each other for a bit. So, it was great to be able to catch up. The two of us talked and updated one another on our lives. But she knew that I was holding back from asking.

"Come on, ask," She giggled.

I couldn't meet her gaze, and I felt my cheeks burning. But finally, I was able to ask, "Who are they, and what do you mean you got me some presents?" She laughed and said, "I figured you would be a hungry wolf here. They were done on the other property, so now, they are ALL yours! They're Bjorn and Carl, brothers from Sweeden."

I could feel my mouth starting to water. Thoughts swirled in my mind. *They're all mine?!* An uncertainty rose up and Kay patted me on the shoulder. "They're great guys and hard workers. So, don't let the dreads fool you!"

When she said that, Bjorn came in while laughing and talking in Swedish with his brother. It sounded as though their language had its own melody. The melodic tune stunned me since I had never heard this language before. There was an atmosphere that felt light and free as they entered, and a joyfulness wafted from them.

My eyes were glued to the two of them. They looked completely different from one another. But both looked yummy to my aching groin. As they got closer, I studied them over and took in their bodies and their clothes. The first thing that I noticed was that they both had roughed up hands and were covered in dirt. However, that was all that they had in common. Bjorn was tall, skinny and had big blue eyes with dirty blonde dreads. Besides that, this guy had a baby face, even though he was the oldest. There was barely any facial hair, and I could see that he had a curious look in his eyes.

Next to him, Carl seemed like he was the opposite since he was just a little taller than me with a nice wide muscular frame. Not only that, but he also had dark brown dreads and a small dark brown beard. Now, he was the kind of guy that I would see as a lumberjack.

His hazel eyes locked on me, and I quickly broke our eye contact. *Why was I feeling so nervous? Could he sense what I was thinking?* I thought.

Eventually, after a couple of hours, it was time for Kay to go. My voice felt parched from all our talking and as I led the way to the gate with Clyde running at the front and Kay in her truck behind, a pang of realization hit me. I would be with these two alone! After unlocking the gate, I gave Kay one last tight squeeze goodbye as I saw that she had that evil glint in her eye. "Have a GOOD time!" She said as she winked and drove out of there leaving a trail of dust. Once Clyde and I got back to the cabin, I saw that the boys were settling in on their newly flat spot with a nice-sized tent set up. The two came down and met up with me and Clyde. It was time for me to get my boss lady side on.

So, I stood up straighter with my hand on my gun and I gave them a breakdown about how we must always carry a gun and that there are sensors throughout the property. When one goes off, we have to check them all. Besides that, I gave them a walkie-talkie to share. This was a great way to know who's doing what and if something terrible comes up, we would say, "Everything is golden." Which means, everything is going to shit! Once all the explaining was complete, the three of us hopped on the four-wheeler and drove up the mountain while Clyde happily ran in front. The breeze felt great as I drove the four-wheeler while the two boys sat on the backside and held on. While I showed them the property, I explained the water system, the tanks, and how everything worked along with where the property ended.

Then, it registered. These two might not know what I need them to do. I racked through my brain, and it clicked. They would be helping me every step of the way. *Ahh, yes! That's how it is to have minions,* I thought and grinned menacingly. I cleared my voice once we stopped at the top. Then, the explanation came from my lips. We would be doing a lot of bucking, de-leafing, and checking the water. A sigh of relief came from me as I thought about how I wouldn't have to deal with 99 plants all alone anymore. Having helping hands was going to make a huge difference. My mind wandered once again to what else I could get them to do. From that, an evil grin overtook my face yet again. But I quickly shook it off. It was supper time. I let the boys stay with the plants de-leafing them while I rode the four-wheeler down.

Clyde was surveilling the area as we made it back down and when he saw that I was walking towards the house, he got a little hop in his step. He knew what time it was, and it made me giggle with his little jump. "Yes, I know. You'll get some food once we get in!" I told him.

I felt puzzled because I had to cook for more than

myself and I felt like I was out of practice since I'd been living on the mountain for so long. Then it hit me, *Soup is a way to go! It's easy, quick, and usually can fill you up if you add the right stuff!* As usual, Clyde didn't want to leave my side. With Clyde at my feet, I added vegetables, lentils, and bouillon to a big pot. The smell wafted into my nostrils, and I got excited, not taking in how hungry I was.

By that time, I called them down with our handy dandy walkies. The two made it down shortly after I called them. As I scooped up their bowls and then mine, it felt a bit awkward. *How do you have small conversations again?!* I felt like I was a newbie to socializing. I wasn't used to having people, let alone strangers in my bubble hidden away from society. But the tension let up quickly since the two were easy to get along with and I saw that Clyde seemed okay with them. *That's always a good sign!* Plus, seeing how these two were hard workers added respect to the mix, especially seeing them work together. My mouth started to salivate, but not from the food. I quickly shut those images down and came back to reality.

Then it dawned on me that we haven't established nicknames. "Okay, you two. We need to have nicknames when we use the walkies. We do this for our own protection. So, my nickname on the walkies is Red. Now, what do you guys want to be called?" I asked as I stared at the two. Both of them looked at each other and then they grinned. "Well, Carl pretty much already got a name from someone who couldn't read his handwriting," chuckled Bjorn. Carl sighed and said, "Yeah, River…"

"Did you want to use that then?" I asked as I thought, *that was an interesting nickname. But I guess mine is just a color. So, who am I to judge?* "Yeah, it's fine," Carl responded.

Then, Bjorn chimed in, "Call me Oso! It's Spanish and it means bear and my actual name means that too!" Now that nicknames were chosen, it was time to do the nightly routine.

The sun had gone down and since we were finished checking on the sensors, it was time to say goodnight. But I still had a hunger. This time, it was a different kind of hunger. I knew that the two were up in their tent, which added a clenching desire within me, and no matter how long I lay in bed, sleep wouldn't come. Only the aching pain grew more from the thought of wondering how good they would taste. My body was radiating with heat, and I knew that it wouldn't be quenched, other than with sex.

After about 30 minutes of tossing and turning, I finally gave in. Clyde stared at me quizzically as I dressed and strapped my gun to my hip. But once he saw that, he jumped down and wagged his tail repeatedly as he ran to the door. Just like that, I was at their tent and my heart was pounding. *What am I doing!?* I thought and I was hesitant to do anything. But Clyde destroyed that by just barging into their open door.

Bjorn popped his head out and had a surprised look on his face. Then, in an instant, he understood and quickly invited me in. I made it obvious that I wanted to stay with them since I had a sleeping bag and a pillow with me. From that, one thing led to another, and I ended up becoming part of a sandwich with these two delicious Swedes. Before it got too heated, I said to them, "This is going to just be fun for a month or so. No strings attached, okay?" Both the boys looked at each other and then nodded their heads in unison. That's when the fun times began for the rest of harvest season.

Once the trimmers came, things between the three of us were still hot and heavy, which left some of the trimmers in shock. But they liked me, so they ended up accepting that those two were my boy toys. Since I had trimmers to take care of, I had turned into a trim mamma on top of harvesting. Being a trim mamma means that you're in charge of feeding everyone, checking on their trimming skills, and then weighing the buds. Besides Clyde, there were the three of us and ten trimmers. So, it was a full house! During this time of the season, Kay came down to help as well. Since Kay and I were back together, noon time turned into Bloody Mary time. This was something that we reveled for. It was our treat and it kept us pushing forward when the two of us were feeling burnt out from the long season.

As the days passed, Carl and I tended to connect a bit more than Bjorn and I. My mind couldn't quite understand why either because when I look at Carl, all I think about is just a pretty boy. But I guess he blew that stigma away since he was also a hard worker. Butterflies fluttered in my tummy as I spaced out thinking about this and immediately, I waved it away. It was time to focus on my work! Reality came back and I just realized how much work would need to be done for us to finish on time! Oh, good old 12-hour days!

CHAPTER 5

I Have Lost Myself! (Present)

Once I made it back to Cali, I was bathed in happiness. Even though my body was in such pain, I was thankful to finally be here. After a bit of arguing with Kay, I was able to get her to drive me straight to the property where I could start being helpful. She stared at me with worried eyes even though she had given in to my desires. The only reason she agreed was that she knew that Carl was there and that I had good ole Clyde by my side.

As we rolled up, Carl met us at the gate with an unwavering smile. Then, Carl and I waved goodbye to Kay, and I quickly jumped on the back of the quad. Clyde gleefully began running alongside and sped past the quad. As my body bounced from the road, my head was pounding, and my inner balance felt wobbly. But I didn't want to let Carl know how much pain I was really in. So, I ignored it. *I mean, I'm a strong woman, I can withstand anything, right?* However, once I hopped off the four-wheeler, I think he could see how much pain I was in.

He stared at me with a concerned glance. But he didn't say anything. My whole body vibrated from the ride. I still felt like I was shaking and each time a wave of pain came with it. I had turned into a slug as I tried to swallow down the pain. But that didn't work. My body felt frail and all I could think was, *why can't I be normal?!* I tried to brush off the ringing in my ears and the waves of pain while we headed into the cabin. But with each step, it was becoming harder and harder to stay composed. Clyde gave Carl several licks and waved his tail frantically as we walked into the cabin.

Once I was inside, I put my stuff in the bedroom and let my body relax on the couch. It felt as though I had just finished a long workday. Carl scanned over my body and took in the tinge of yellow and brown where the remains of a big bruise were once on my arm. In no time, Clyde was at my side and moved my hand out of his way, so that he could have his head on my lap. A serene feeling came over me, and I began petting him while trying not to think of the pain. I closed my eyes as a single tear fell from my eye.

Reality faded away and I ended up in my safe dark place where I felt no pain, no emotions, just a feeling of calmness and of just being. It was there where I knew that this pain and the feelings that I was going through were *but a moment.* I could feel a reassurance that all of this would be over. When that happened, I must have passed out because I came to from hearing Carl moving pans out of the way. My head felt groggy at first and then I remembered that I was back in Northern California. A sigh of relief came out of me as I saw Carl. I was thankful to be alive and that I got to see this scruffy looking guy again. His ripped jeans were covered in dirt and resin from the plants. As he got closer, I could see that his skin had a layer of dirt as well. But under that dirt, he had a golden tan from working hard in the sun daily.

My loins came to life, and I quickly tried to silence them. *Quiet, you!* I thought to myself. Just as I did that, Carl turned to me with a plate of yummy food. The aroma filled the air, and I could smell dill and some garlic, which made me begin to drool. I didn't realize just how hungry I was until I was staring at the food. My plate didn't last long before I devoured it. After scarfing down the meal, it was time for bed and my body felt heavy, even more so than before. My eyelids were becoming difficult to keep open and I hadn't thought about much, which seemed strange to me. However, my mind was not as it once was. Things that used to cross my mind didn't anymore. It felt calmer within me than I have ever had before.

We talked about sharing the bed beforehand since we were friends with benefits in the past. So, it didn't seem like a big deal to us. Plus, I wanted someone close besides Clyde with how much grueling pain my body was in. Once my head hit the pillow, I was out. The darkness swallowed me whole and held me in its grasp. I welcomed it and felt the heaviness of pain be lifted. My body relaxed and I was in a serene solitude where I could just focus on nothingness. At the same time, within my body it told me that there was work that was needed. In that same moment, my inner self quickly got to work like it was a factory creating something new.

Smoke came from the chimneys as the belt started moving again. There were many hands all around working away on the belt and using all kinds of tools. I'm watching from above and I try to peek at what they're working on. But I couldn't see anything from all the long stretchy bleach-colored arms and hands in the way. Just then, a loud horn echoes in the building, and I abruptly come to. My eyes open quickly, and my heart is pounding. I analyze the room and realize that I'm back in northern Cali. I had forgotten... again. A big sigh came out of me, and I was able to relax next to Carl with Clyde at my feet.

The next day the sun's rays came down on all the plants and the wilderness. A feeling of stress lifted, and my heart reveled in joy from being back with these plants. The smell and the feeling of being encased by them soothed me and helped my body relax. It brought me to a state of tranquility where all stress and much of my pain dissipated. However, no matter how much I tried to hide it, Carl saw when I was beginning to get into excruciating pain. When this would happen, it was as though my body didn't want to cooperate any longer. It had only been an hour working with the luscious green ladies, and my body started to betray me...

A stabbing pain came from my neck, which connected down to my arms. From that, I was having trouble just grasping the leaves. I could feel everything slipping away. My freedom, my independence, they just vanished. But since I was stubborn, I didn't want to stop, not yet. I took a deep breath and kept working away by grabbing the Fiskars, slow and steady. However, that didn't work for very long, and Carl saw me shaking. A hint of concern washed over him as he came to my side.

"Do you need some water?" He asked hesitantly.

"No, I'm fine," I said bluntly as I kept trying to use the scissors. I kept thinking, *it's only been an hour, I can't stop yet. I should have started working earlier. I should have left home right after the hospital!* At that moment he gently grabbed my hand and said, "I think you should rest, and then we'll see how you are in a bit." My eyes held a glitter of defiance. Then it quickly vanished. I knew that he wanted to help me and that he wasn't doing this to be mean or controlling in any way. Besides that, I couldn't fake feeling good anymore and this hurt my pride since I was doing such a mundane task.

My gaze locked on the scissors and my useless hands, then back at him, and with a big groan, I gave in. Carl gave me a ride back to the cabin on the four-wheeler and told me just to walkie him if I needed him. No matter how much I tried to get Clyde to go with

Carl, he was adamant about staying by my side. I knew that Clyde could sense my pain, and he wanted to be there for me. The accident made him into an overly protective guard dog who didn't want anyone near me when I felt like this.

So, Carl took off, while the two of us headed inside. I was thankful that we had set up the computer near the bed already because after putting on a movie and starting it, a wave of exhaustion overtook me, and I was thankful to be able to rest in bed. Clyde with his brilliant eyes stared at me with patience. He acted as though he was on duty, hopped into the bed, curled up with me, and nudged his face under my hand. He wanted to make sure no one would harm me as vulnerable as I was.

Now, it didn't last long before the tiredness pulled me and soon, I was asleep. Sleep had become my friend, and it was something that I could feel was helping my body heal. I usually wouldn't fight it when it came knocking on my door. However, I didn't have much else to do. So, that made it a lot easier to accept it. But after an hour or two, I woke up. As I moved just a little to my side, my whole body erupted in pain. A seething sound came from between my teeth and Clyde picked up his head and stared at me in worry. He crept closer and put his nose under my hand. This made me chuckle. I knew he was trying to help.

I mustered enough strength to sit up and the world started spinning. Immediately my eyes shut and I and told myself, *this is not happening. I'm feeling a bit better. My vision is okay.* As I thought this, the pain eased a little and after waiting a few minutes, I opened my eyes once again. My world wasn't spinning anymore, and the pain had lessened. So, I slowly walked to the computer and put something on. Right at that moment, I could feel that I needed something. So, I listened to that feeling which led me to the kitchen. My tummy felt hungry, but it was an unusual hunger. So, I kept following that pull and ended up taking out two celery sticks. This went on for a bit with me going back and forth from the bed to the fridge until I had eaten the whole celery stock! I felt a bit better after that. In actuality, my body felt so good that I wanted to venture back outside and start working.

Since Carl was at the back property, Clyde and I walked up the mountain. My head began to thump wildly. So, we had to take many breaks before we could make it to the greenhouse. A sigh of relief came out of me as we got inside. The smell was potent, and I could feel my body unwind. While I stretched out my arms, I could hear birds singing as they passed by. From the atmosphere, I started to feel lighter, and a small smile played on my lips as I began de-leafing the gigantic plants. Every touch of a leaf gave me a jolt of stimulation that seemed to course through my body. This place was just what my body needed.

The pain let up even more as I began working away.

It wasn't until an hour or so that the pain started to come back with vengeance. I could feel between my shoulder blades this dull pain that kept getting harder. From that, it was becoming difficult to move my arms. While I was trying to find a way around this, Clyde started to bark frantically, and my stomach dropped. *Uh-oh.* I thought as I started to feel guilty for sneaking out, and I could already tell that my fate had been sealed.

The sound of the quad thrummed louder as Carl got closer. Once he reached the greenhouse, Clyde stopped barking and did one last happy bark. When he did that, it felt like I just got told on. *Aww man...* I thought and I knew that I couldn't play off this pain. When Carl came into the greenhouse, it was as if a heated wind came in with him as he took me in with one glance. I could feel the anger seeping off him within seconds and my gut dropped even further. *Yup, I was in trouble.* After a good scolding he brought me back to the cabin and made sure that I went to bed.

"But it's so... boring to stay here, and I... can help!" I stammered since I was having trouble thinking of my words. He took a deep breath and then calmly said, "I have about an hour of work to do on the backside. How about you wait for me here, and we can watch something together?"

I lit up with elation! It wouldn't have to just be Clyde and me. But I didn't want him to know how happy I was to hear that. So, I managed to say, "Okay." In a low tone. He stared into my eyes as though he was trying to see into my soul. Then, just as quickly, he left. My heart missed a beat. *Was he always like this?* He reminded me of the wind with how quick he is and how he comes in with such a fierce feeling. He was just really good at filling the area with his presence. It left me breathless.

I regained my composure and put on a show while I patiently waited for him to come back. Clyde jumped up and crawled onto my lap. Once he did that, I automatically started petting him while a show of no importance played. While the show played, I kept looking at the clock in the room. My patience wasn't the best. Finally, after 45 minutes, I heard an engine roar outside. My heart leapt in delight as I heard it coming down the hill. A bubbly feeling began, which I was able to relax by the time he came in.

Sweat dripped down his face and into his tiny beard. My whole body felt like it was on fire as I stared at him. *What is wrong with me!?* I thought as I tried to get a grip on myself. He went to the sink and washed as much resin off of his hands as he could while telling me that he was going to take a shower. When he looked my way, I just nodded my head, and my cheeks started to flush. *Calm down, we've done more than just this before.* I thought as I tried to hush my thoughts when he walked to the bathroom.

Just then, I remembered that this was the first time it has been just me and him working together. We had been in Peru and Bolivia together, but that was different. Being together alone on this mountain so far from others and having a homey feel to it was an unknown territory between us. My heart beat rapidly as I thought of him in the shower. But I instantly shut that down as I picked out a movie for us to watch. Not soon after I heard the nozzle creak as it turned off, and Carl walked to me in the bed with drops rolling down his flat stomach. My eyes grew wide as I took him in. I calmed myself as he jumped in the bed with his boxers on. My heart kept spinning and getting to cuddle filled me with such glee. Besides that, I was filled with a warmth to my bones. The movie played while I was fighting with my rampaging hormones. It didn't last long before our bodies became intertwined, which ended up in sex.

While I was healing, there were days when Carl gave me some cranberry juice and would have me sit outside while he worked away on chopping pieces of wood. I couldn't complain when he would do this. So, he got me to stay in one spot while he got to work, a win-win. Each time he would swing the ax, I would feel the adrenaline pump through me as though I was on a roller-coaster ride. Seeing a man being able to work hard was definitely my thing and he had the whole package.

One day, while I had worked more than a couple of hours, our water guy came to put water in our tanks. The two of us would usually talk because we got along pretty well. But this day he stared at me in concern. He could see that my pupils were different sizes. Since he's an old military man, he had seen a lot of battles, and seeing my eyes like that made him tell me adamantly to go lie down. I felt like I had to surrender and reluctantly I walked slowly back to the cabin.

After the first month or so on the mountain, I was finally able to get Carl to let me drive into the bigger town by myself for a big grocery run! That meant 30 minutes without a chaperone! I was overjoyed and giddy with the new independence after many days of struggling from day to day. As I took off on the twisty and windy roads, I was starting to get nervous with how the steering wheel started to feel and I slowly pressed on the brake. That's all it took for me to spiral into the side of the cliff with the back-end bumper.

My heart plummeted and felt like it was going to pop out. Relief washed over me since I hit this side instead of spiraling off the cliff. *What am I going to do? I can't go back empty-handed, and I won't have this freedom again!?* I thought in a panic. I took a deep breath and started up the truck again. It went smoothly to get out of the tiny ditch and then I kept driving towards the big town. Determination roared to life for me to accomplish this simple task and I wasn't going to let this get in my way.

Once I made it back to the cabin with all the food, I began to put the groceries away as fast as I could. Then I went up to the top of the mountain and started working away with the plants. It wasn't until 30 minutes to an hour later that I heard the four-wheeler roar to life. It sounded more urgent than regularly and hastily Clyde and Carl were looking at me exasperated. I could tell from Carl's look that he must have seen the truck's bumper, and my heart dropped. "Are you okay!? What happened?" He asked in a worried tone. My heart felt warm with his concern and the lie easily flew from my lips. "Aww, thank you! I'm okay. It was a hit-and-run when I was inside the store. So, it's okay." I had a genuine smile on my face.

It wasn't until later when we brought the truck to the mechanic that we learnt about the truck's brakes. They were so bad that he highly recommended that it should not be driven until that was fixed. A light bulb went off within me. *It wasn't my fault. It was from the brakes on the truck.* I thought with comfort that I wasn't completely broken.

It was becoming a routine with me sneaking up to go work with the plants. Then, Carl would have to put me to bed and sex was usually involved. Along with that as part of the routine, sleep had become my best friend. It called to me frequently. But it wasn't until one day when we went into town that everything changed.

There was a free box of kitties, and my heart melted. *What we need are some mice hunters!* I thought as I looked at their enormous eyes and heard their high-pitched meows. It didn't take too long to talk Carl into it, and we ended up going back to the cabin with two newly adopted kittens.

Since I felt a responsibility to take care of them, I didn't sneak up the mountain as much. This probably made it a lot easier for Carl's nerves and better for my body since I wasn't trying to work more than I could. These little furballs took a lot of my attention and they helped me not fight with Carl when I had to go lie down. However, Clyde wasn't too happy with them, but he dealt with the two kitties. He wanted all my love and wasn't thrilled with sharing. Nevertheless, we were beginning to get into some kind of routine.

But then one day, we got a call from the sheriff who had found me after the car crash in Wyoming. He told me how glad he was that I was alive and that he was shocked that I was able to talk. Suddenly the words came from him uncontrollably, "You fractured your neck, and you were so close to becoming paralyzed for the rest of your life!" Once he said that, my body dropped to the chair next to me and I was filled with full gratitude. *Everything could have been so much worse!* Tears streamed down my face as I listened to him a little longer and I finally said thank you for calling. I hung the landline back up as the tears kept pouring down.

Soon after that, Carl came back, and he saw me in a wreck. So, I told him what had happened. He grabbed me and held me tightly. Then he told me that I was okay, which ended up bringing the water works out of me again. When I finally calmed down, we started to watch something as I laid my head on his chest. A wave of comfort rippled over me as I had him there. This was when I truly needed someone, and he's been there so many times for me when I needed it. Carl has been my savior from myself and from feeling alone.

That feeling of lust crawled within me, and I started to caress his chest with my fingertips. My eyes roamed up his face and I could see that he had that heated look in his eyes too. I gave him a passionate kiss and he gently touched my cheek. That night ended in covers everywhere and mixed feelings of love and lust. I had trouble comprehending what to do after that. Once we woke up the next day, we cuddled for a bit and then, out of the blue he said, "We should get married."

A gasp escaped me, and I was in shock. *How do you respond to that?!* He kept talking then, "I almost lost you. I don't want that to happen again." He said this in a quieter tone with uncertainty at how I was to react. But my heart melted as he said it, "... Are you sure?" *I'm glad that he said it. But this was crazy!* I thought as my mind raced. *He's a Swede. He'd have to give up his world to be with me?!* I couldn't understand. But finally, after fighting with myself in my head, I said, "Let's do it." My heart felt like it grew and heated up, which turned into us rolling around in bed, kissing, and another round of lovemaking.

Once I had told the news to my parents over the phone, they were sick with worry. So, it didn't take them long to come for a visit. Their first thoughts were that I was badly damaged in my head and that marriage should be the last thing on my mind, especially to someone that they heard next to nothing about. But once they came, their thoughts changed. My parents could see just how much Carl cared for me. He wanted my parents to like him. So, he even fixed a fancy dinner for them and gave them space with just me. This ended up putting their hearts at peace. They felt good to leave me in the hands of such a nice and capable guy. My heart soothed as they said this, and a feeling of satisfaction rushed over me. *Was I hoping that they would like him? I guess so...*

CHAPTER 6

Traveling Outside the Norm (Past)

The winter months came and my parents were in the Sunshine Keys RV Park in Florida. This was their go-to spot during the cold seasons. I said my farewells to them and Clyde as I hopped on a plane and flew to Lima, Peru, to meet up with Carl. My heart pattered as I thought of him and my mind kept trying to talk sense into me. But I ignored my mind and followed my impulse. I pushed forward and took this big leap to another country just to meet up with this guy. My nerves were a bit on end since I had never traveled out of the country alone. It felt like my emotions were on a roller-coaster ride with the feeling of being excited mixed with anxiety, worry and then back to happiness.

Once I arrived in Peru after about seven hours, I was exhausted. My Spanish wasn't up to par and hearing the people speak made me recognize that I was far from home. I wasn't sure what was happening due to a language barrier. From that, my mind could feel that I was slipping away from where I needed to go. Until I started following the flow of people and found my backpack. My gut started to knot as the sun was setting. *How was I going to get to that hostel?* I thought in anguish. Just then, an older man came up to me about a taxi. I knew that I should have tried to find a ride elsewhere. Since this was my first time in a country alone, fear enslaved my judgment, and I took the expensive ride. The prices looked average to me. But I didn't take into consideration the price difference in another country. It felt safe going with this company since this guy was inside the airport and came from a genuine business with a desk.

The sun was completely gone by the time I got to the hostel and after ringing the doorbell several times, a young sleepy man came to the door. Before my flight, Carl and I had been keeping in contact on Messenger. So he had told them that he had a friend coming. The guy who had answered the door looked at me with tired eyes and said, "Bonnie?" I quickly nodded my head, and he ushered me in. The dark hues made it difficult to see anything. It was pretty late, so it made sense that it was dark. Yet the feeling of the place was relaxing. When we got into the dorm room, I could see that everyone was passed out in bunk beds that were scattered everywhere.

"Carl!" The young man yelled when we were in a room full of bunk beds. Carl popped out of the bottom of one of them with slitted eyes. The tired guy nodded goodbye to me and took off. Now, I stared at Carl in shock as he tried getting me to sleep in his bed in his half-asleep state. That pissed me off right away. My emotions were fuming. *What the hell?! We are just friends!* I thought angrily as I shrugged him off and climbed to the top bed. My mind kept thinking of the text that he had sent me which took me about an hour to decipher. Carl's writing skills in English need a lot of help and, finally, when I was able to understand what he meant, I was pissed.

Bonnie-

Hey there! You know you coming here is that. We are meeting up in Peru and it's nothing. We are what we are. So, when you're here it's just that.

See you!
Carl

I finally understood that he was saying we were just friends, nothing else. *So, why in the hell would he invite me to his bed when I first arrived in Peru!?* Fumes of anger came off me while I lay in the top bunk bed thinking this over. But after a while, I took a deep breath and was able to get myself to relax enough to sleep.

The next day, I woke up feeling groggy, and my eyes slowly adjusted to the new place. Dark curtains covered the windows and only a slit of light streamed in. I looked where Carl had slept, and now it was just an empty bed. *I guess it's time to get up.* I thought as I stretched out my legs and arms in the bed. Then, excitement overflowed. *I'm in a new country!* My mind began to imagine all the new experiences that I would have. I felt like a little kid waiting for candy or popcorn excitedly before the movie started.

After getting dressed and then brushing my teeth, I met up with Carl at the bar which is also the breakfast spot. The two of us reconnected and I never mentioned that text he had sent me. My mixed feelings stayed hidden, even from myself as we traveled through Peru for the day. Once we made it back to the hostel, Carl ventured back to the room for a bit to have some alone time.

Then, as I was hanging out at the bar, a tall good-looking guy came up to me with a cute smile. I was good at picking up on what kind of person someone is when I meet them, and this guy rang, being a nice one. His short brown hair matched his structure with his sculpted chin and charming dimples. One look at him and my first thoughts turned into animalistic ones. *Jeez! I need to calm down!* I thought to myself as I could feel a blush creeping up my face.

"Hey! I'm Max! I was wondering if you'd like to try some of the local food with me?" He asked with a bounce in his step.

I scanned the bar and saw that Carl was on his way from the dorm. "Hang on a second!" I said to Max while I held up a finger and scurried over to Carl. I explained what was going on and Carl quickly said in a rough tone, "He's asking you! You can go!" My heart dropped. *Did I do something wrong?* I get the feeling that Carl is jealous. But that can't be since he told me in that damn text that we were just friends.

So, I dismissed it and went to the street market with Max where he divulged what he wanted to do as we both were munching on our meals. "So, I have been talking with a local and found out about these two guys that can give a 3-day trip to the Amazons. But I need more people to come along in order to be able to do it! It's going to be amazing! Camping out in the Amazons, trying local food, and staying out in nature! What do ya say? Do you wanna join me?!" He asks gleefully.

"Well, it does sound great. But I'm traveling with my friend Carl. I can't just leave him." I stammered.

"That's great! He can come too! The more the better!" He responded in a cheery tone, which bothered me. My heart sank and I noticed that he just wanted to experience the adventure. But I abruptly let that feeling go and explained to him that once we get back to the hostel I'll talk to Carl.

I was hesitant about going on the trip. That's a big leap into the unknown and especially with a young guy that I just met. To make matters worse, Carl said, "You get to choose!" with a scowl on his face. So, it was all up to me. All the decision making was on my shoulders. So, what better way to explore a new place than by following that impulse of mine. *It was time for us to go with this guy we hardly knew into the jungle. Great idea, right!?* I chuckled as I thought how crazy this was. But I didn't back down from the decision.

The three of us ventured by boat for a day or so to a small village. It was mostly locals on the boat, and it was a good thing that we had bought hammocks prior to this ride since that's how everyone slept. The people lined up in rows of colorful hammocks that swayed while the boat moved. We were even given piping hot rice as our meal. My emotions were starting to feel like a high as I stared at the beauty surrounding us the further into the Amazons that we went. The cool breeze felt inviting and refreshing as we got closer to the little village.

Once we got off the long chipped blue boat, the locals gawked at me. It was obvious that they weren't used to seeing a white person. *Hmm… Well, this is new.* I thought as I seemed to have turned into an exotic animal to them. A short dark brown man with calloused hands came walking towards us and ushered us to follow him. This guy was one of our guides and brought us to his home. His house was a shack with a tin roof and there wasn't much for walls. It felt like it wouldn't be able to withstand an intense wind. But here it stands even through the downpouring rains that they can have. While I skimmed the room, three of his kids ran around giggling and stared in awe at me.

I ended up having a bit of fun playing with them

and they showed me interesting papers with drawings and some words. The children were around 3-8 years-old and they were bursting with energy. By the time that everything was in order for our trip, I had bonded nicely with the kiddos. They were even teaching me Spanish! Another local with the same build as the first one came into the house and then we were off. My nerves were on end with a mix of excitement and fear. We had our bags packed and loaded up on a canoe with a motor right away. It felt like everything was happening so fast and just like that, we whizzed out of sight. As we faded in the distance, the air whipped in my face which cooled me down and felt pleasant.

Our surroundings quickly changed as we puttered on through the Amazons. As we went further into the jungle, the trees towered above the water and spiderwebs were overtaking the side of some of the hanging branches. I saw a mass of spiderwebs wadded up on two trees that were almost the same size as the trees surrounding it! It took a couple of hours, but we found a great spot for the night. Since it was the rainy season, we had mosquito nets put around our mats and every night we were flooded from our newly found area. So, it turned into three nights in different spots within the Amazons.

One of the days, I was ecstatic from adrenaline. We had learned how to catch fish with machetes, and we caught eight! When we did this, we would wait in the flooded stream and with a quick whack, we were able to get them one by one. It was an eye-opening experience that left me feeling cheery and amazed at the whole situation. Another time while we were floating down the river, our guide who was driving suddenly stopped. Without saying anything, he crept up a tree and hopped back into the canoe with a sloth on his arm. My jaw dropped and all three of us stared in wonder. He let us touch it and its fur felt wiry and oily. Then he asked if we wanted to eat it. A feeling of horror jolted through me, and I immediately shook my head no as I waved my hands.

That night, the guides took us on the water, and one of them without a word just jumped into the pitch-black water. I didn't understand what was happening and I was left in confusion. Just then, he came back up and this time he had a baby caiman! So, the three of us got to see the baby up close and touch its smooth scales. Our headlamps shone on the little body, and I could see the fear in his eyes. His breathing was quick, and I had an urge to put him back. Just like with the sloth, the tour guides asked if we wanted to eat it and, of course, I said no.

Another one of the days we went swimming in the black water within the Amazons. Other parts of the Amazons had murky brown water, which wasn't safe to swim in. This water reminded me of sludge, and it didn't look inviting at all. But the water we swam in was pitch black and if you were close to the surface, you could see through it a little.

The days were scorching. So, being able to swim felt rejuvenating. But it didn't last long since we saw a tarantula on top of the water and in an instant it dived downwards. When that happened, both guides rushed back to the canoe. The three of us were oblivious. However, seeing them freak out was a great heads-up and we followed suit.

After our time in the Amazons, Carl, Max and I headed towards Iquitos on a boat that was filled with locals, cows, and chickens. It took about three days with us sleeping in our hammocks and wandering to the top of the boat to take in the scenery. However, my heart dropped when I noticed that no food or water had been given to the cows and their bodies were showing that. The hips protruded and at one point, one dropped to the ground and never got back up...

At one point, the locals' strapped a rope around that cow's neck and dragged it to the side of the fenced area. It broke my heart to see how they dealt with the animals in general. The chickens that they had on the top deck had feathers all crumpled up and they lived in their own excrement through the ride in tiny boxes. But I was able to brush it off since there was nothing that I could do. This was their way here, a part of their culture.

Once we made it to Iquitos, we talked to a hostel worker into letting the three of us use their attic as our place of stay, which meant we got to pay dirt cheap for our stay and we got to use our hammocks hanging from the wooden rafters. It was airy up in the attic and the roof was just a metal lid. However, the breeze felt welcoming and cool. The walls were boards, and the room was wide and open. It felt like we had our own little hideout.

One of the days, Max had gone away. So, Carl and I were left alone, which ended up getting hot and heavy. We intermingled on the mattress that we had on the ground. But while we were intertwined, Max strolled up the stairs and spotted us in action. His eyes filled with shock to find us like that. His initial thought was that we were just friends and nothing else. However, once he walked in on us, he learned that wasn't true.

When Carl and I explained this to Max, it was something that both of us easily dismissed, like it was no big deal. Although my feelings towards Carl felt like they were becoming more intense. My heart hammered and my breathing picked up as I started to notice that the two of us were growing closer on this trip. So, I felt that I needed to extinguish those feelings. One of our days here, I found a cute local boy that I had a night with as Max and Carl went and explored together.

Eventually after an hour or so, Carl had found me with the local boy and helped me get back to our hostel since I was pretty drunk. *Ohh, me and my problem with alcohol.* But before I could part ways with the local, he gave me a deep kiss and then let me vanish with a Carl that seemed to be holding back his fists. Carl finally got me back to the attic and he seemed a bit pissed. His body was fuming with anger as he escorted me away from the guy.

It was the next day after that night when Carl abruptly said to me, "We should go our separate ways." I was taken by surprise and a weight dropped in my gut. *I traveled here so that we could travel together. Now he wants me to go solo?!* I thought angrily. But after contemplating it, I agreed with him. Then I would have some space away from him and not have to think about these feelings that kept popping up. It felt like Carl wanted us to travel separately so that he could protect himself by pushing me away.

With my hurt pride, I wandered in Peru on my own. However, since I'm not shy to talk to new people and I'm easy to get along with, I made friends easily at the hostels that I stayed at. A few of those hostels that I stayed at were known to be party hostels, which meant a heck of a lot of drinking. So, every night turned into a lot of drinking and partying.

One of the places that I was at, I met two girls, and in an instant, we hit it off! Amanda was from Australia and the other girl was Bri, who was from the States. As I sat there at the table eating breakfast, the two of them strolled up to me and sat down. Amanda's long wavy blonde hair moved in the breeze and her wide smile was contagious. Our eyes met and I couldn't help but smile back. Bri sat next to her with a hop and a loving smile as well. Her unruly curly brown hair yelled attitude. But that wasn't the feeling I got from her though. I could tell immediately once we started talking that she was easy to get along with.

"So, where ya from?" Asked Bri in a cheery tone.

"I'm from the States, South Dakota," I said, and I felt a connection right away with Bri since we both were from the USA.

Amanda sat there quietly as she listened to us talk more about where we were from and the differences. About an hour passed and, finally, Amanda and Bri looked at one another as if they were agreeing with just their eyes before Bri asked, "So, do you wanna go to Colca Canyon with us?" I was surprised and I hadn't even thought about Colca Canyon, let alone know anything about it. However, I wanted to have new experiences and since the three of us got along so well, I couldn't see any reason not to go with them. So, I instantly agreed, and their smiles grew bigger.

The next day a buzz for adventure came to life within my body as I packed my bag and hopped on a bus with the girls. It was an excruciatingly long trip, and we were packed elbow to elbow with the locals. The heat was building up from us being tightly squeezed in the bus. Each bump reverberated the bus and I thought that the shocks were absent. But finally, after the lengthy ride, we made it to the beginning of our hike. My head was swirling from the heat in the bus, and I was ready to get fresh air.

My body ached from being cramped for so long. I took a huge inhale once we were out of the bus and bathed in the sunlight. As I stretched my arms up, a feeling of exhilaration engulfed my body. It was time for a new experience! Now, I had no idea what I was getting myself into with this hike and soon I would find out that I wasn't fully prepared for the warmth. The sun pelted down on us with each step we took down the canyon. While we progressed downward, the three of us were good at staying at the same pace. It was surprising that we were able to keep conversations going for most of the walk as well. However, my body was beginning to feel the aches and the red rocks below my feet were starting to feel worn-out. My head felt like it was giving off fumes from the heat. Because of that, there were a few times that I doused my head in water. Finally, when we got to the bottom, and I was encased in satisfaction.

Once we reached the base, the beauty of the towering walls surrounded us. The place where we were going to stay at had a pool with water cascading down a man-made waterfall. My body yelled for the water. So, I decided to jump in once I put my swimsuit on. Having that icy cold water on my body helped the aches and pains. A calm sigh left my lips while the three of us just relaxed in the water. While I did that, the other two sighed in unison with me. So, we gawked at one another and burst out laughing. We had done it, we made it down Colca Canyon!

After a night well rested in the comfy beds, it was time for us to start our journey up the canyon! I took a big gulp and started getting dressed with the thought of the climb upwards. Every step I took left me with a jolt of pain throughout my legs. As I started putting on my shoes, it became apparent that the bottom of them had MELTED! It was so hot on our walk, that my cheap knock-off shoes had dwindled to an uneven rubbery mess. *Woah.* I thought and chuckled. *Well, it seems I'm hiking with these misshapen shoes.* I sighed and just let it be. There was only one way out, and that was up.

When the three of us met up before starting to head up, I told them about my shoes while I bent my foot up for them to see. Their jaws dropped and both of them asked if I would be okay. In that moment, I let go of the problem. Besides there wasn't anything we could do about it right there anyways.

After that trip and then wandering to Bolivia, the girls and I went our separate ways. While I followed my wanderlust, I kept meeting new friends throughout Bolivia along with experiencing drunken parties at hostels. As I traveled, Carl kept showing up in the same places, and my first thoughts were that he must be traveling like a lot of the other people were from the hostels. So, I didn't think anything of it. When I was in one of the hostels in Bolivia, I started to click with a guy from Spain. But then Carl showed up and I dropped the nice-looking Spaniard in an instant and ended up sleeping with Carl. My feelings kept pulling me back to Carl, even with all the guys that I met while exploring the countries.

The two of us kept in contact as we traveled separately. Then, one day, as I slept, Carl showed up at the hostel that I was staying at in Santa Cruz, Bolivia. He searched in confusion with a hostel worker for me through many of the rooms. But he had no luck. So, he waited in the lobby and once I woke up covered head to toe in purple and blue dye, Carl's mouth gaped open when he saw me. The night before I was doused in ink since it was carnival time here. It was no wonder that he didn't recognize me in my bed.

My head pounded relentlessly from the alcohol, and I was stricken with guilt that I had stained the bed sheets. But the worker just chuckled and reassured me that it was okay... *I guess that's why they had you sign a waiver before and why that was mentioned in it. I'm guilty.* I shamefully thought.

While I thought of the mess I was, that Swedish boy, Carl coaxed me into going into the swimming pool, with a push. Then, he jumped in after me and began scrubbing my ink-infested body. About half an hour passed, and I was as clean as I could be. But my head was still persistently banging, and my energy was lost. The whole time I felt like I was a child getting scolded while I had to hold still to get clean.

After the pool scrubbing, we cuddled in my bed instead of going out. Since we did that, I swirled in gratitude since my head was still throbbing. I knew that he had trouble staying still. So, I gave him my phone, which had a Thor game on it. It worked like magic, and he was enthralled by the game and was able to stay put. As my head rested on his firm chest, I could hear his heart thump steadily. Right then and there, I was showered in feelings of safety and comfort. Sleep soon took over me with the tune of his heart and I was lulled to sleep by that beat.

We both realized it and once I knew that this was love, I almost ran with fright. *I can't believe that I had my guard down with someone, and I'm not even flinching at the idea that now I'm vulnerable. That is scary!*

CHAPTER 7

What Do I Want? (Present)

Once we arrived back on the property in Cali, an ominous feeling lingered in the air. As we rolled up to the cabin, my mouth fell open. I had left my small truck there, thinking that it would be okay. Well, that was the wrong move. It had been gutted and now it was a junk car. All its' tires were missing, parts of the engine were gone, and the windshield was broken...

I couldn't believe what I was looking at and I just kept thinking, *why?* We scoured the area and noticed that the container had been forced open and from it, old trim bags had been taken out. I had to take a deep breath before looking inside the cabin. As I came up to the back door, the handle had been unhinged. So, I took a big gulp before heading in. I had no idea what I would find. But from the bad feeling that crept over my body, I knew what we would see was going to be heartbreaking.

The door opened with a loud creak and sadness filled my heart. All the pictures that hung on the walls were torn and scattered on the floor. My clothes were thrown around and my comics were all gone. Along with that, we couldn't find any of the guns, which really worried me. It took us about ten minutes or so for us to collect ourselves and as I sat on the bed with tears streaming down my face in silence, I decided that I was completely done with the place. It was time to say goodbye and I had no urge to clean the mess. So, I took whatever could be salvaged and told Carl that we were leaving.

With all the new stress, my head began to hammer away, and I just sat in the car with Clyde's head resting on my lap. Our two kittens scurried around in the back as we headed to town. We drove up to the coffee house, which was busy as usual. Gina would be working, and I wanted to say our farewells. So, I leapt out of the car into the cool breeze which soothed my head from the pain. Clyde followed me and then Carl. The door of the coffee shop was left open for a nice breeze and the music languidly played in the background as we walked in. I quickly saw Gina busily wiping the empty tables. Once she saw me, her eyes shined and we hugged. Then, she said a warm hello to Clyde and then to Carl. She abruptly turned back to me and squealed, "You're back! Yay!"

"Well, actually, we're leaving. We've decided we are done here." I said in a somber tone. Then I explained in more detail how we had found our place and that it didn't sit well in my belly. Her eyes faltered from the news. Then I told her that we are off to South Dakota instead so that we can help my family with their business since they've asked several times. Gina's eyes grew big as I divulged everything, and a big sigh came out of her. "The same thing happened to a lot of growers actually. One of the mechanics was also hit and even the bank got hit! It was a planned mission, and they must've been scouting the spots beforehand. So, it's been a bit off around here…" She said sadly.

One of the mechanics in town and even the bank was broken into?! This left me stunned. *Even the bank!?* I thought. My thoughts started to wander, and I felt an urge to get far away from this town even more so. Gina gave me an overview about what's happening in her life. Then about her family before we embraced one last time. Around that time, the owners of the coffee shop showed up, a couple in their 50s. So, I got the chance to say goodbye to them as well. Then Carl, Clyde, and I headed back out to the van. A feeling of freedom ruptured within my body. I felt lighter and calmer. Working for someone felt like such a burden and now it's been lifted, and I hadn't realized that, until now. My body felt free. Yeah, I would miss my friends. But my freedom had been lost and now I have it once again.

The hour ride was quiet as I sat in my seat gazing out. My mind drifted within me, and I felt solitude as though I was surrounded by the harmonious darkness that I go to so often nowadays. I felt at peace and dissipated all the troubles and anguish that began to come up from our little adventure to the cabin. The pain in my head lifted for a bit. But once we hit any bump, I felt a jolt in my head, and I would have to work on soothing myself again.

We were on our way to the coast so that we could have the not-so-fun talk with the owner. But first, we headed to Kay. I started to feel delighted with the thought of seeing her again. It had been around 6 months since I had last seen her and boy, did I miss her. Once we parked on the street in front of Kay's house, Clyde and I ran out and I knocked on her door repeatedly with giddiness.

She looked out the window, saw our car outside the window, and with a skip, she rushed to her door with her dog, Jasper, at her feet. I jumped into her arms in a warm loving hug. At the same time the two dogs said a warm hello to one another while they both wagged their tails playfully. My mind felt at home as we decided to settle into her place for a couple of days before we planned on heading out. Kay's hazel eyes held a sad glint as I told her what had happened at the farm. Her brow furrowed even more when I explained about all the properties that were robbed.

"That's shit!" She cursed and stomped to the kitchen for another cup of coffee. "It is what it is. There's nothing we can do about it. That's why we've agreed to head to my parents. They've been pleading for my help anyway. So, in a way, it works out." I replied calmly.

She came back into the living room with a smile creeping onto her face. "You're always so good at seeing the good side of things. I'm envious!" She said as she poked my side in a playful act. I squeaked and quickly sat on the couch next to Carl. He had been just watching the two of us interact in fascination. Clyde sat by our feet once I had sat down and with that all-knowing glance, he stared up at me. After an early night of watching a show, the three of us and the dogs passed out. Our kittens purred before they fell asleep in a little pile on the bed. Once my head hit the pillow a wave of exhaustion ensued. I've become overly sensitive from being around any kind of action. So, traveling, seeing the mess on the farm, and then being in a new environment weighed on my head and body.

I welcomed the darkness with my arms wide open. Time for myself was needed, and I immediately ascended into my dark place within where I felt a warm loving feeling of relaxation there. My legs and arms went out wide and basked in the feeling. Golden strings wrapped around my body and overlapped several times on the areas where I had pain. The pain from the fracture in my neck lessened and I could breathe without any more strain. In that same instant, everything went black, and I fully passed out.

We spent the next day picking up food and items for the upcoming road trip. Then, in our spare time, we went back to Kay and hung out with her. After that, we had our not so fun talk with our boss. This ended up adding more anxiety to my already painful head. I felt like I had been battered all day from our errands and I plastered myself down on Kay's couch. Clyde lay below me and kept an eye on everything, making sure that I was safe. He was back on guard duty as I lay sprawled out. Carl and Kay talked while I tried to rest my brain. It felt like it was trying to break out of my skull with each pound that echoed within my head. There was a sharp pain between my eyes and other intense pains were just behind my temples.

My world felt like it was beginning to spin, and I couldn't focus on thinking. So, I was glad that we had finished with errands so I could work on just being. As the pain waved through me, a shock of anger came. *Why am I still messed up?! How long will I be like this?! I want my life back!* I thought angrily. It had been over a year, and I still didn't fully feel like myself. My focus was still troublesome, and I still couldn't get the words to flow out of me. On top of that, I would have an intense and expanding pain in my head that would come regularly from stress, the weather, or overstimulation. Another issue for me was that it was hard for me to accept when some things just didn't click in my head that used to be so easy.

For instance, some of the daily tasks had become lost in my head, and I didn't understand what Carl wanted me to do. Or I had trouble remembering what he had asked right after he had told me. In those instants, I would feel lost, standing there like a forgotten puppy. It felt like I was pathetic, useless, and a waste. *How could someone want to be with me?* I thought as tears began to well up in my eyes. He didn't understand and I knew that. From the outside, I look normal, like there are no issues. But on the inside, it felt like a brutal battle to hold onto who I am or what I thought was me. Pieces of me kept chipping off and then they would be lost forever in that peaceful darkness. I still didn't feel like myself and I had no idea how to fix that...

The next day we said our goodbyes to Kay and headed out. We wanted to get on the road at a decent time so that we could get closer to South Dakota. Now, a new chapter begins in my life and a lump of fear of the unknown comes rolling in. I worked on gulping it down. But pieces of it stayed since my confidence in myself had been cracked away. My independence wasn't fully back and there were times when I would hold a knife to my throat within myself. At times I was my best cheerleader, and then other times, I was my worst enemy. The inner battle was an extreme place to be!

CHAPTER 8

USA Road Trip (Past)

Since I was on the edge of death, my outlook on life and my goals have changed (or broadened). I mean, I have always secretly been a hopeless romantic. But the last time I acted upon that, was at 15. Now, brewing in my mind are these feelings of a heart-hammering love that feels surreal. These feelings started to bud for Carl before the accident. *So, at least I know that it's not this brain injury warping my thoughts. Yay! What do you do when you can't follow your urges, when someone brings emotions out of you that have been dormant for years (10 years to be exact)? Well, I guess you get married and go on a road trip for your honeymoon!*

Before we had left Northern Cali, we had bought a tan Astro van and built a wooden frame within it so that we had a place for all our stuff in boxes underneath it. On top of it, we had a mattress rolled up with a strap making more space for the two kitties and Clyde. My mind began roaming off to space as Carl took over the wheel and then sleep ensnared me in a much-needed rest. Since my accident, sleep pulled at me a lot more. Each time, I felt a sense of healing flood through my body. When this would happen, it was like I was looking at myself in someone else's shoes and watching the healing from within.

Once I woke up, my eyes slowly glided to Carl. The sun hit perfectly on his body, promoting his tan muscles and great figure. It felt like drool was going to start coming from my mouth. But he must have felt my gaze because he looked my way, and abruptly, I turned the other direction to avoid eye contact. My cheeks were scorching hot with a rosy tinge to them. I finally calmed myself and noticed the wonderful sky outside. The bright blue sky held streams of white that once were clouds and the closer we got to Yosemite National Park, the more beauty overtook our view.

As we got closer, my jaw dropped. The tall, towering mountains gave a magical feel to the place. Trees were stretched out throughout the area giving a splash of lush green to the gray stones. I rolled down the window and could feel the cool breeze, which made me giggle from how free I felt. Excitement ringed in my ears and I wanted to yell. Being back in the wilderness felt like my home, my true calling. I could feel the little girl inside of me getting giddy thinking of all the fun adventures we could have here. The smells of the trees engulfed my nostrils as we headed down the street. This just added to me feeling even more alive. All my senses were getting a treat!

After driving a bit and paying for a pass, we found a spot near the tough Yosemite Falls trail that we wanted to do. Trees stretched over the car, giving a nice shade with the cool breeze. It was the perfect spot for our kitties and us to prepare for the hike. Since we had such a good spot, we didn't have to worry about leaving the cats. So, we settled with having them stay in the car with the windows down. Then we snapped on the kitties' leashes and connected the two with a carabiner since they are the worst with teamwork. The two furry kitties stared up at us while we began packing our daypacks. Clyde could sense that an adventure was soon to happen. So, he wagged his tail adamantly with his tongue hanging out.

My heart began to crumble, and I started to fill with doubt. *What if I can't do this?* I thought and just as I almost talked myself out of it, Carl spoke up. "Hey, you got this! Let's go!" and then he reassuringly touched my arm. That's all I needed to dissolve that doubtful feeling and off we went.

My breathing became rough, and a pounding echoed within my ears giving me even more pain in my aching head. The path was steep, and each step forward was at an incline. Tears streamed down my face and then I remembered. A feeling of gratitude came over me as I thought of my backpack. I stopped and took a deep inhale. *Okay, body. What do I need?* I asked and right after that, I could feel the answer. So, I grabbed my water bottle from my tiny backpack and proceeded to drench my bandana before putting it back on.

Carl ultimately noticed that I had stopped since Clyde was waiting for me. They were further ahead of me. But after drenching my bandana, I felt more refreshed. However, a feeling of anxiety ran through me that this hike was going to be long and intense. This was just the beginning, and I was already getting the stabbing pains in my head.

Once I reached Carl and Clyde with his sincere eyes, I said, "Don't wait for me. It's going to take me a while to get there. I'll see you up there when I get there." Carl stared at me uncertain about leaving. But he knew better than to argue with me since he had quickly learned about my stubbornness from when he first met me. So, after he gave me a warm hug and a kiss, he said goodbye. I petted Clyde on the head swiftly after he gave me some licks and off they went.

Relief flowed over me. It felt good that I didn't have the pressure of anyone waiting for me. I was able to go at my own speed without any worry. But a feeling of loneliness poked out its head. *How could he?! Now you're dealing with this all alone!* Screamed my mind. But I let that thought quickly dissipate. This was my choice, and I knew this was a battle that I had to take on by myself. I'm the only one who can use my legs and I'm the one that gets to choose what I do with myself. A feeling of determination consumed me, and I began hiking upwards.

My head wasn't too thrilled with my idea. So, I had to rest about every 5–10 minutes. My body was aching, and I was puffing with a cherry-red face. Tears kept running down my face as I took some sips of my water and this whole time while taking on the trail, I was fighting within. That mind of mine kept telling me, *I can't,* and then my body would just say, *You can do it. It will just take some time.* This kept going on back and forth within me.

Until finally, I felt like I had enough. So, I was trying to decide if I should head down. But at that moment, a hiker was coming down from ahead. He took one look at me and said, "You're doing great! There's just a bit left." When I heard that, relief filled my heart and then I knew I wasn't alone. Just getting that helpful push is all I needed to keep going forward. From there, I had to keep taking breaks and almost in sync, another hiker would show up to give me some encouraging words to help me keep pushing on. My heart filled with gratitude and my tears spilled into joy instead of pain.

With every step, I started saying a mantra in my head, *Slow and steady wins the race.* Eventually, I made it to the first stop with a great view of the lower falls. People were scattered around and once I saw the cascading water, my heart leapt with happiness and a feeling of accomplishment. There was only a little bit left until making it to the top from there. But this last part would be the hardest with more of an incline! After resting, I began heading towards the top and saw Carl and Clyde coming down. Just seeing the two of them lit something within me and I couldn't help but smile.

My cherry cheeks felt scorching hot, and I knew that my eyes showed just how exhausted I was. But seeing these two gave me some energy and the feeling of belief in myself ignited. I could finish the trail.

"We waited. But we wanted to make sure everything was okay. So, we started heading back down." Carl said matter-of-factly.

I could see his eyes held concern. He wanted to make sure that I was alright. My heart felt a pang of warmth from his words. A smile played on my lips as I squeezed his hand saying, "Thank you! I'm glad that I get to do the last part with you two!" and then I quickly patted Clyde on the head as he started wagging his tail frantically.

The three of us started toward the top, slow and steady and with many breaks for my sake. Until finally, we made it! Through red eyes and a tear-stained face, I saw the magical view of the half dome, which reminded me of a world of fantasies and wonder. Besides that, the roaring of the upper falls distracted me from getting lost in just the mountain. I followed the sound and there, the upper falls pelted down with such force.

Yet another feeling of relief ran through me, and my whole body felt a comfortable warmth from within. *I did it!* As I stood with my eyes closed and lived in the moment, I felt at peace. I just proved to myself that I can, and it has only been half a year since my accident! *It's possible! You just have to believe!* I thought to myself as I sighed in fulfillment.

On our way back down, the darkness followed our footsteps as we treaded down slowly the rocky path. My legs almost gave out a few times from exhaustion and I had to keep telling myself that it was alright. To top it off, the darker it got, the more glued I was to Carl's arm. I couldn't differentiate where the ground started and where the horizon was. My equilibrium felt like it was becoming shaky from the absence of light. So, my balance was crap, and after about 10–12 hours, we made it back to our car!

After a well-deserved sleep in the van with the two of us cuddled and the animals snuggled up to us, we rolled up the bed. We checked everything and the animals before we headed out for our next adventure!

A contrast to the sunny yet cool Yosemite National Park with its vibrant plants spread throughout is Death Valley with its desolate land that has its own beauty. The sun showered down on us. But since we were in the middle of this desert area, Clyde got the chance to run in front of the car. Once we stopped, he was smiling from ear to ear and happily barked. His breathing was heightened. Drool dripped off his tongue as he licked us frantically when we came out to see the Ubehebe crater. I gave my excited Clyde some love as Carl hooked Oscar and Ayasha together. They were about 6 months old and most of their life had been on the road instead of in one spot. However, they still weren't good with teamwork when it came time for them to be attached together.

Right next to where we parked, we could see the deep hole in the ground. It left me amazed to think that this was created by a crater. *The world is such a fascinating place. If only we would take more time to enjoy it.* I thought as I sat down on a brick wall while the cats played on the rocky ground. The two made a game of the leash that was attached to them. When one moved forward, the other would whack at the moving string and pounce on it. This made me giggle. While I hung out with the kitties, Carl and Clyde wandered down the crater to see just how deep it was. When I stared at the hole, it was hard to tell the depth until those two walked down there. Then it became quite obvious that it was really deep once they were down there. They looked like tiny ants as they began climbing back up.

There was a lot to see in Death Valley and since we came here during the wintertime, the heat was bearable. In contrast to the heat, was the chilly nights. So, we just stayed for a couple of nights. But during the day, we would go on a new adventure or see a different part of the Death Valley. This place held its own feeling of harmony. There was so much to explore, and this was just the beginning of our trip.

On our road trip, we stopped in many states, and while we did this, I kept getting lost in my mind. At times, I had trouble focusing on the physical world. My reality tended to feel more like it was within me and not on the outside. But this was beginning to make it difficult to keep my connection with others, especially Carl. He didn't fully understand what was happening to me and that sometimes my brain wasn't connecting to the right memory, or the words that I held within wouldn't come from my lips. This alone was frustrating since I couldn't grasp the words that I wanted to say. I could feel them on my tongue. However, I couldn't get them out of my mouth.

Now, how do you explain these kinds of things from outside of your inner world? It's difficult when you're going through problems with the brain, especially since there's still so much unknown about traumatic brain injuries. Plus, the affects for many people are completely different from one another. At times, Carl would get mad at me when my brain misfired. When this happened, my heart would sink.

It wasn't his fault, and I knew that. I mean, I didn't fully understand why I couldn't comprehend things that come so easily to others. The brain is a fickle thing. There were also times when I would get angry at him, which was hard for me to understand. I would ask myself, *why had I lashed out at him?* But I guess it was just the first year of us together.

Once we made it to Arkansas, we followed the curvy roads that turned into gravel roads. Finally, after driving for a while surrounded by the greenery, we made it to my aunt's home. My body was throbbing in pain from the drive. But I was excited to see my cousins. Chris and Joe were around my age. So, I hung out with them when my family and I came to visit. Chris and I have the same birthday as well, and I've always felt a strong connection with him.

I was ecstatic to meet everyone since it had been some time. My heart thrummed with joy, and my aunt let us keep the kitties in her garage. Once we got our furry family settled in, Clyde, Carl and I stepped into the house. My aunt Therese gave me a tight squeeze even with her tiny physique. Her long brown hair hit me in the face with her excitement. All I could do in her suffocating embrace was focus on breathing.

It was around Thanksgiving time, and we made it just in time for festivities. I scanned the room looking for the two boys. Many other cousins and my other aunt came and welcomed me. Even Joe showed up a little later with his short black hair. But still no Chris.

Carl was helpful the whole time, helping my family prepare some last-minute appetizers while I talked to many of them. Our eyes met, and I saw how happy he was to be useful. My heart felt full, and it was nice to be around a lot of my family once again. But I kept having an inkling that something was a bit off. That's when Chris showed up with his glazed eyes and a hollow look. He stumbled through the door, and I stared at him in worry. I quickly gave him a hug and asked, "Are you okay?" He mumbled something incoherent and then started laughing. I brushed it off and let him be for a bit.

Then, a little later, I talked with Joe since those two are brothers and they practically do everything together. That's when Joe told me how Chris had been popping pills and had been losing himself along with it. Suddenly, about that same time, I saw Chris showing a video of how doped up he was and how he just passed out while he was standing. When I saw that, fume was radiating off me. *How could he laugh at himself like that?! How could he enjoy being so messed up that he can't even function?!* I thought this and started connecting how I was struggling with being functional. But here he is, throwing it away for some kind of high. He doesn't realize how grateful he should be for the freedom he has.

It felt like I was going to burst with anger as I pushed his phone back into his hands. I stormed out and into the room we were going to sleep in for the night. Tears ran down my face and a roaring head pain came with it. I couldn't understand him and it hurt me because I wasn't able to explain myself or help him with his struggle. *This is just too much stress.* From his actions, I could see the pain his mom and Joe were feeling as well.

While these thoughts rolled in, pain crumbled my thinking, and I finally listened to my body. My body hit the bed with Clyde by the side of the bed. As I lay there, I began taking deep breaths and focused on breathing, until I was able to fall asleep. The rest of the trip in Arkansas was short lived since I didn't want to be around that stress. So, after a day, we headed back out to our next destination.

When we rolled up to New Orleans, curiosity coursed through my veins. All the stories that I had heard about New Orleans made it sound like it's a one-of-a-kind place. So, we meandered the streets after we got the cats comfortable in the van in a nice cool spot. Clyde, with his own excitement for new places, joyfully wagged his tail as he walked by my side.

Music boomed in the air, and we followed it, finding a band playing in front of an important-looking white building with pillars. One played a saxophone, while the others had a guitar and some sort of drum. While they played, each person had a smile plastered on their face as they danced. The area vibrated with their energy and the crowd swayed and moved with the infectious music. As we crept closer, my feet started to do a two-step dance and then I twirled as I laughed. Carl looked back at me and smiled. The two of us danced while we had a happy Clyde following my steps.

Just as the sun set, the city dramatically changed for the nightlife. The three of us took to the streets once again and got our fill of the nightlife from visiting loads of bars. While we did this, a pain inched further into my head, and it kept getting stronger, piercing the only thinking that I could do. But I didn't want to give up. I wanted to stay with Carl and Clyde. I wanted to party and have fun like the people surrounding us.

So, I proceeded to drink, which was the worst thing I could have done for my brain. It was soon after that I had blacked out and, in that mix, my mindset plummeted to a dark space. There, it felt like Carl would realize that I was broken and would no longer want me. Fragments of myself with slurred words and glazed eyes came to my memory. Then the words came out like vomit when I told him to sleep somewhere else that night.

In the middle of the night, the feeling of panic engulfed me, and I sat up instantly. My eyes scanned the car and pleaded that Clyde and Carl were nearby. But there was no Clyde and no Carl. My heart started to hammer away. I scrambled through my brain, trying to put the pieces together as to what had happened. Then a foreboding feeling that I had pushed him away came. My head was pounding, and I started to feel like I was swirling… *I had to find them.* I thought. So, I looked for them as if I was a lost child calling out their names. After what felt like hours, I gave up and went back to the van. Then, soon after that, they showed up and I felt my nerves eased.

Carl looked at me skittishly and had trouble keeping eye contact. "What happened?" I asked and he looked at me quizzically. "You kicked me out. So, Clyde and I slept in a park nearby." *How could I be so selfish and inconsiderate? I pushed him away to protect myself. What is there to gain from doing this?! And they had to sleep out in the cold! Jeez Bonnie!* I thought in a rough tone. "I'm truly sorry! I don't know why I did that... Are you okay!?" I stammered as I tried giving him a hug. "It was cold. But I had Clyde. So, it was okay." He replied. He was hesitant to hug me. But finally, he gave in. We embraced for a bit as my eyes began to water. *Why on earth would I be so stupid to do such a thing?! He's someone important to me. My best friend, my soulmate.* I thought angrily.

After that escapade, I made sure that nothing like that happened again on the trip. My insecurities had redirected my actions, and I had thought that I didn't deserve him, which fueled me to backlash at him. It was my defense mechanism that began pushing him away before he could do it. It was in that instant that I realized just how stupid that kind of mental state was. But this way of thinking and acting lays dormant in my subconscious which stems from my upbringing and past experiences.

We visited around 22 states on this road trip and some places were harder to deal with than others. For instance, one of those times we were in the middle of nowhere and I was passed out lying on the bed as Carl was driving. He decided to pull over so that he could sleep as well. It wasn't even ten minutes until a guy in a rusty big truck rumbled up to our side with three gigantic dogs in the back. He had a shotgun hanging above his head and he stared at Carl with penetrating eyes. "You can't stay har!" He yelled as he began grabbing for his shotgun. Carl put up his hands immediately and said, "Okay, we'll go!" So, he got back into the driver's seat and took off. I came to from my sleep quickly when I heard the yelling. But it was as though the whole scene was fragmented.

Most of the trip, I kept going in and out of a fog as I sat in my seat. During this time, Carl drove the twisty roads in the smoky mountains. I was having trouble focusing. So, to help clear my head, I rolled down my window. The fresh air felt great. A gust of wind hit me straight in the face with a pine scent. *Home.* I thought as nature engulfed our path. Some tall mountains surrounding us along with the green fir trees and other variations of trees was immersed in my view. My head began to clear more. But as we started going up and down, I could feel my stomach threatening to hurl. I quickly sat back down in my seat and closed my eyes. It felt like it was time for a break soon.

A non-comprehensive sound came out of Carl's mouth as he stared at me with a frustrated glance. Whatever he had said, it didn't compute. My brain was having trouble connecting the dots and words were failing me. I couldn't grasp any of the words that I was thinking of. Carl didn't understand and it wasn't his fault. But that didn't change how I felt. A lonely tear trickled down my face as I stared out the passenger's window. He had been getting upset with me lately since I couldn't understand little things and the weather was affecting my ability to have a conversation. *What is wrong with me?!* I thought and wished to be back to normal. However, I knew that was not my reality.

We started driving up a tall mountain and the road kept spiraling. I held onto my head as we made curve after curve and finally, we made it to the top. A deep breath escaped me that I hadn't realized that I was holding. The tension in the car was still there. But it had lessened, and Carl looked at me and asked calmly, "Are you ready to cross the grandfather mountain bridge?"

I looked at him with big puppy dog eyes and nodded my head. A fog began to encroach, and Clyde stayed with Carl so that I could have both of my hands. Our cats stayed in the car since this wouldn't take too long. I could see the mile-high swinging bridge through the fog and as we walked closer, I could see the drop! It hung high above 5,946 feet and this area is a nature biosphere reserve. The fog made the area feel ominous and for some reason, I was thankful that I couldn't see below, which would have added to my stress of being on the swinging bridge. After creeping onto the bridge,

I was spent. My whole body pulsated in exhaustion. Stress level was an all-time high for me, and so after that, we left. My head was throbbing. I thought that it would have been okay since I was out in the outdoors. But the weather had other plans for me.

After a night in a cozy cabin up in the smoky mountains, we headed to Tennessee and found an interesting cave with a waterfall within. This was called Ruby Falls, and my eyes grew big once we had walked through the cave to the water cascading down. They had lights that would change colors on the falls, which added a different atmosphere to the place. I felt starstruck by the beauty. The wilderness has so many hidden gems and every place we found on our trip brought an excitement to me along with a feeling of gratitude. Even with my head injury I'm still able to relish in the moments. I'm still able to travel and see the abundance of nature throughout the states.

A feeling of gratitude washed over me and calmness along with it. My pains subsided for the moment, and I was able to just BE in the moment. The water rushed down with a serene sound that felt like it was talking to me. I closed my eyes and imagined that I was submerged in the water and that it was healing all my pains and aches. Then, I took a deep breath and let it out as a smile slithered onto my face. A surge of happiness came, and I stood there, just holding Carl's hand in silence. Life was good.

Next stop for us was to meet up with more of my family. I have some cousins and an aunt in Ohio. Since we were driving through, we might as well say hello. Plus, more of my family gets to meet this mysterious Swede who has stolen my heart. My aunt Ally with wide-open arms grabbed me and squeezed me tightly. The breath escaped me and finally, she let go. I dropped back down and saw that she was grinning from ear to ear. She was looking over Carl and our furry family in one big glance before saying, "Welcome! You have a place to stay for the night! So glad to meet you, Carl. How was the drive? Tell me everything!" She hooked her arm around Carl's and led him into the kitchen while I stared dumbfounded.

What just happened? I thought and then I shrugged it off. I grabbed some of our gear and the animal food, and headed into the room that we would use. Then, while I did that, thoughts about how Ally is really good at talking came to mind, which made me giggle. *I wonder if he'll have a chance to say anything.* I laughed once more and started unpacking.

When I made it to the kitchen, the two were chuckling while they worked on food. The smell wafted to my nostrils, and I could feel that my tummy was empty. A low growl came out of me and the two stared at me for a second and then began to laugh. "I guess you're hungry, huh? Good thing we're making food and it's just about done. Sit down!" She said in a commanding but happy tone.

Once we had food, more of my cousins had shown up and the dining area was filled with laughter and voices. The chatter grew louder and ended up turning into a blaring noise. At first, I was filled with happiness. But it was beginning to dwindle down. All of it was becoming too stimulating and after eating, I told everyone that I had to go lay down. Each movement I took back to the bedroom was getting heavier. The pain was coming and the closer I got to the bed, the more surges of pain that came.

My arms were out and I just dropped onto the bed. I felt drained all the way to my core. It felt like I had run a marathon or hadn't slept in weeks. And all that happened was just from being around family... I felt sick with myself. *I couldn't even handle being around my family. Why...* I thought as I stared up at the ceiling and if on cue, Ayasha came up to my face with a *Meoow!* Her bright blue eyes stared into mine and my anger diminished. I grabbed her and hugged her close. Clyde rubbed up against my leg and let me know that he was there too. A chuckle rolled out of me, and suddenly in my peripherals, I saw Oscar climbing the shelf in the room with his one leg dangling off. He quickly got his feet under him and climbed further. A sigh of relief came out of me that he was safe. Then in that moment, I just realized that I wasn't alone. Some of my pain eased from that thought and I was able to fall asleep with Ayasha and Clyde next to me.

After a few more stops and adventures, we ultimately made it to Oregon. My eyes took in all the overgrown greenery from outside the window. The moss and trees clung to the mountains, and everything had a mist to it. The trail that we had stumbled upon was something from a fairy tale. Water trickled from above on certain parts, while in other places we had to hop over streams of clear water. The cool breeze eased any pain in my head, and I was able to do the Punchbowl Falls hike with ease. While Clyde, Carl, and I wandered the well-paved path, the sun peaked out behind the clouds. Its' rays stretched long and broke through the puffy white clouds, bringing a glow to the area.

Some of the trail involved us to walk right next to the cliff's edge, which made my heart sink to my stomach. But I was able to keep pushing forward, even with the fear of heights. As we kept following the trail, a feeling of peace overcame me with each step. It felt good to be fully surrounded by nature again. I had missed it, even though it hadn't been that long. However, each state has its own atmosphere to it. I could sense that this place had a more otherworldly feel to it, which calmed me for some reason. It wasn't something that I could explain to anyone. So, I lavished the feeling in silence.

After walking the winding trail, we made it to the

gigantic powerful waterfalls. It seemed magical as I stared at the cascading falls. From the force of the water, it looked as though it was going to burst. The area felt serene and untouched as Clyde, Carl, and I sat there taking in the charm. Everything felt right and my body seemed to be happy along with my head. What a good trip here!

As we wandered together on this road trip, I could feel a gap between Carl and me. Since I had trouble with saying what was on my mind and he had trouble understanding my hardships, we kept hitting a wall. When we argued, an uncontrollable pain would take over my brain and thinking was the last thing that I could do. So, trying to form a sentence when I was in that state of mind was difficult. Having this barrier between us worried me. *What if we can't make this work out? What if I'm forever broken where I can't form my thoughts into words?* These kinds of things came to mind several times as we drove through the states. It felt as though Carl had turned into my safe space, my lighthouse through a storm, and having that safety gone would break my heart.

But as the world goes, we must push on and keep trying.

CHAPTER 9

The Path to Healing (Present)

It felt somewhat nice but at the same time, it felt like we fell into a blackhole. South Dakota tended to hold me prisoner every time I came back. I was happy to be around family and friends. But my heart wanted to explore the world, I wanted to see so much more than this place. However, I had a pull that was telling me to help my family, especially after seeing the farm wrecked by poachers. That experience in Cali opened my eyes and I found that I wanted a little more time with my family and friends with my new hubby. It had been a year since my accident and still, I didn't feel fully like myself. It felt like there was a void within me, a piece of me that was still missing. *Maybe being here, where I grew up will help me find what I have lost.* I thought as my eyes scanned the luscious plants outside the windows at my parents' home. The bright hues of my mom's flowers brought more life to the yard along with her garden decorations. The waterfall in the pond was soothing and helped relax my nerves.

Reality kicked in once I realized that I had spaced out. *It's back to work,* I thought as my fingers started typing away on the computer. I continued to work on documenting the pile of paperwork for my dad's roofing company that needed to be put into the computer. A pit of despair started to grow within me. I couldn't understand why. But it felt like this paper seemed never-ending as the days went by.

Carl was helping my dad by working on the rooftops with my brother and all the other regular contractors that my dad had. Each day after a long and stressful day filing the papers, scheduling jobs, ordering materials, and sometimes collecting the checks, I would crash into bed and sleep hard. My head felt like it was on overdrive by the time the day was over. At times, it felt like my brain was trying to break out of my skull. It acted as if it was caged and couldn't be set free.

After a long day, my body would be in excruciating pain and my neck would be roaring in agony. I couldn't look down over the computer for too long and doing that for days on end brought a feeling of having an unhinged neck. My fractured neck was something that I kept forgetting, and this was its way of saying, *listen to me!* So, when that would happen, I would sometimes give in and rest. This was usually the time that I would either go to the gym or stretch.

Since I was able to work whenever I could, that meant that I could drive into town anytime and work out. The days when I got to do that, it felt like I was soaring back to my freedom. But then there would be those days in a month when I would be in so much pain that the bed turned into my sanctuary. I could hear the panging in my ears coming from my head and the last thing that I could do was to think. Plus, I can't forget that I was a workaholic! So, even when my body was in piercing pain, the need to keep pressing buttons or making calls was there. I wanted to prove that I wasn't broken to myself and everyone else. *But at what cost?* Panic swept in when this would happen. I wanted to be able to have control. But I was still broken, and I usually forgot that…

Other times when I wasn't in pain, I almost felt normal. Besides missing a piece within me and having trouble keeping conversations, I acted and looked like a normal person. My writing skills were good and recording the documents when I took breaks for my neck. It was like I became hyper-focused when I was working. But when it came to regular conversation, that was problematic. Then, I would have to use my brain to converse and mine was still not fully there yet. My conversations ended up being short and a lot of daydreaming was involved.

Finally, I noticed that piece of me that was missing within me was my ego. It was still there but not where it usually resided and not as big. That's why it was difficult to fully feel like me. I felt detached and not part of this world. Since that was missing, it was easy for me to drift away from reality and go to my safe space that was within me. This tended to freak people out as I would daze out often. But I didn't care. During those times, it didn't bother me what others thought while I spaced out to my hidden paradise. When I would do this, the feeling felt familiar and a bit like home. I would feel at peace every time that I wandered back to my tranquil place of darkness.

"Dani... Dani!" Carl yelled and I instantly was knocked out of my daze. I was back to my computer and now I stared back at Carl. "Are you okay?" He asked with a concerned look. I nodded my head and went back to typing. He rested his hand on my shoulder and said, "Maybe it's time for a break. The sun is shining. Why don't we go to the Japanese garden with Clyde?" When he said that, my eyes sparkled with delight. That place was my little sanctuary that I relished going to when I was in town.

My body felt like it was vibrating with eagerness as we walked towards the Japanese garden. Clyde wagged his tail, and he stopped suddenly, then started to follow a smell in the breeze. The three of us walked towards the wooden open doors and strolled into a world full of cherry blossoms, manicured lawns, and stone structures. My whole body felt at ease once we were in and a calmness swept over me. *This is what I needed. A step away from the busy life.* I thought as the cool breeze picked up.

I took a deep inhale and could easily smell the cherry blossoms. The vibrant pink petals and flowers took over certain parts of the path as we meandered through hand in hand and an excited dog. He pranced down the path before us and patiently waited until we caught up. Then, we decided to sit down under a stone pergola with vines climbing above us. It felt magical and I rested my head on Carl's shoulder. My heart filled with love and gratitude for this moment. I could feel my inner self say, *yes. This is the way.*

As we sat there in silence, I basked in the feeling of just being. Clyde sniffed around but didn't go too far. He felt he always needed to be close, especially after the accident. Finally, the words came out from my lips, "Thank you." Carl could tell that I needed a break and since he knew me so well, he brought me to the perfect spot. My body started to feel rejuvenated and after an hour or so, we headed back to my parents.

I've gotten better at listening to my mind and body during this time in South Dakota. Along with that, I've learned what they need and how to help myself heal. Being busy helped my brain remember how to function and for my body, exercise was great. Besides that, breaks were much needed. At first, I would have tears pooling out of my eyes from just trying downward dog. But I didn't give up on myself! I kept pushing! Every day when there was a chance, I would go to the gym and work on yoga, Pilates, the machines, or TRX.

I even had a trainer to help me stay accountable at one point. Now the people who knew about my accident and how recent it was were amazed at all the things that I could do. But what they didn't know is that it wasn't easy. Battling with my mind regularly was tough and I know that it was my stubbornness that helped me to move forward.

This is especially true on the days when I felt like just giving up. These days, I would ask myself in a gentle voice, *what do you want to do today? It's okay to rest.* I had learned to talk to myself as if I were a kid. During these times, I became my own best friend, and found that you have to become your own cheerleader. Only you can take the steps that are needed to get better.

But there were times when I was overwhelmed with the workload and the stress that came with the stack of jobs that were never-ending. I was just one person and on top of that, my brain was still healing. There were days where I was in so much pain throughout my body that I couldn't move. Other times, I couldn't remember the littlest things if I had not written them down. One time, I had forgotten to pick up Carl at some point, which shattered his heart. He must've not realized just how badly damaged my brain was since he never even called to remind me.

While typing away during another long working day, I heard the footsteps of someone on the porch. I promptly looked up and coming through the door were my favorite nieces (only), Gabriella and Jenivive. Both giggled as they came in. Just then, it hit me! It was after 4 pm and we said that we would hang out together. I had completely forgotten. An overwhelming rush of emotions came over me as I looked over my work. That's when I decided to close the laptop after saving the spreadsheets. *It's time for family. This is what I need.* I thought as I got up with a light thumping in my head.

When these two sisters came around, their silliness would get the better of them. They would play off each other and make me smile or laugh even more. We got into Gabriela's car for our little trip to town. As we rolled up to Falls Park, a gasp came out of me. The beauty always amazes me and it's in the middle of the city! The waterfalls cascaded down with such force that the sound echoed throughout the area. As the water rippled and roared, I could feel it wash away my stress and calm me. Only a feeling of easiness was left as I gazed around the greenery. The cool air whipped around as the three of us walked the paths around the falls. My head was still pounding. But now, it was less. I could be in the moment.

I took a deep breath in as we watched the falls from the bridge before proceeding on the walkway. The two giggled in front of me while they chatted, and I was lost in the moment. I was submerged in all the sounds of the birds, the waterfalls, and the wind. In that instant, I felt safe and as though I was in the right place at the right time. My mind and body connected with happiness and being out in nature. All I wanted to do was lay in the grass and soak up every minute. So, I did just that!

As the girls talked, I headed towards the grassy

patches and found a place to lay down. The two were stunned that I had disappeared. Then, immediately they found me sprawled out in the grass. Their laughing filled the air as they approached. My eyes were shut, and I savored all my senses being filled to the brim. A smile spread across my face and then I opened my eyes to stare up at them.

"What are you doing!?" Jenivive yelled through giggles.

"I felt like I wanted to be in the grass. So, I'm in the grass." I said nonchalantly as I closed my eyes again.

"You're so weird!" Giggled Jeniveve as she looked at me.

Later, the three of us settled on heading to the downtown area for supper and it's a good thing too! My tummy started rumbling and my head began to throb with pain. The heat had gotten to me and now I needed water. *Not yet.* I thought to my head as the pain began to grow. It felt like the happy times were starting to fall through my fingers. As if, the fun times would be over. But I tried to let that feeling go and messaged Teddy to meet up with us at Sushi Masa, one of my favorite spots!

Once we stepped into the restaurant, a feeling of familiarity overcame me. I felt excited and saliva began to pool in my mouth. We sat down and quickly after, Teddy showed up. A genuine happiness came out of me when I gave him a huge hug. Teddy is a great friend who's a big guy with his curly mane, which is a mix of his hair and beard. Even his laugh booms with a contagious glee. When he walks into a room, it's as though he brings in a pleasant torch with him. Besides that, he reminds me of a huggable teddy bear, thus the nickname Teddy!

"So, how are you doing? You seem a lot better than when I saw you after the accident." He said as he met my eyes. I happily answered, "Yup! I'm doing A LOT better! Of course, my memory is still a bit off and sometimes I slip on my words. But, I'm feeling a lot better!" My smile reached my eyes and made him feel assured that I was okay. Then he told me how he and some of our friends were worried about me. But it seems that wasn't needed.

My nieces, especially Jenivive, had fun talking with Teddy and eating the unforgettable miso soup. We all laughed and lived in the moment. But as reality came back, so did my head pains. We said goodbye to Teddy as the three of us headed to the car Then, the unavoidable words came out of me to the girls. I needed to rest. My heart felt suffocating. *I don't want to go.* I thought. But I knew myself better. If I don't rest now, my whole body will be against me, and I might have to stay in bed for the whole next day. It grew silent in the car once I told them that and it felt like the air got heavy. Gabriella understood a bit more than Jenivive since she was older. However, both of them still had trouble grasping that I wasn't back to being me.

Weeks go by doing the long workdays and working on being normal. Just then, my phone rang, and it was Peggie! She told me in excitement that Strawbale Winery was having an event there and that we should go. So, brimming with enthusiasm for the idea, I told my mom and my hubby. Once Peggie drove to us, we all piled in my parents' truck and drove there. It wasn't too far from us since it was in the countryside. After parking, I could already hear the live music booming. My body vibrated with anticipation and the closer we got, the louder it became.

Besides the music, there were farm cats and chickens, which added a homey feel to the experience. But, since I had my accident, alcohol and I weren't friends, especially wine with sulfites. I had my own glass and wanted to be back to my past self so that I could just enjoy it all. But the hammering came back and this time it was angry with me. I had drunk more than a glass of wine and I couldn't handle it. The feeling of being caged started to consume me and I fought it by drinking another glass even with the pain. I was fighting what I already knew, and I just couldn't give it up. If I did, it felt like I was giving up my freedom. So, the next day and even the day after that, I was useless. Lesson learned…

Some days later as I was working away on the computer, my dad came in beaming with joy as he stared at me. He kept looking at me and my concentration was lost. I took a deep inhale, stopped typing, looked up at him, and then asked, "Can I help you?" I was a little perturbed, but I brushed that off. "You've been doing such a great job! I'm so happy that you're here. And that you're... alive." He said as his smile faltered. "I almost lost you. That was horrible."

My eyes softened as he said that, and I put the computer down and walked over to him. I gave him a big warm hug, but this whole interaction was strange to me. My dad and I usually butt heads as soon as we are in the same room together. So, this was different. But I savored it, and I think I didn't realize how long I had yearned for it. Finally getting any kind of recognition from my dad was something that I had always strived for, and it was a near-death experience, which ultimately gave me what I wanted the most from him. My emotions went haywire. However, I had to keep it together. I was the responsible one, the one taking care of so much in the business. After a long hug, we awkwardly stared at each other and then I went back to the couch to keep working while he yelled for my mom in a cheerful tone.

Now, a great thing about this kind of job is that there's no work in the winter. So, when wintertime came it meant that we could hit the road and start a new travel journey. My heart pattered with the thought as we headed out. I could feel all the stress leave me as we drove away from the blue house. It was just the two of us and our whole furry family!

CHAPTER 10

Fall in Love with Sweden (Present)

After a year, the busy times were going to be put on pause for us as we packed our bags. It was time for us to leave South Dakota and start our journey to nature-filled Sweden, my hubby's homeland! I felt eager to learn of all the places that I would get to see and experience. Plus, I would get a taste of Carl's life before he moved to the USA to be with me. There was this deep desire within me to find out as much as I could about him and the best way to do that is to go to his country.

All the possibilities scattered before me within my mind and a feeling of happiness poured over me. Once we said goodbye to Clyde, the cats, and my parents, we were off to the airport with my friend, Mavry, who was such a helpful gal. I sat in the front so that I could talk with her and reminisce on our party days and the days of high school. But while we did this, I could feel a huge gap in my memory. It was hard for me to fully remember, which brought panic to me. In that same instance, a wave of piercing pain came, and I silently endured it while she talked. I let our conversation die since I couldn't think any longer.

My world spun and I hadn't realized that my mind was getting an overload of memories. However, it was just pieces of several memories mashed together. So, it was hard to comprehend what was happening and every time I tried to grasp a memory, it flew out of my hands. This brought a boiling anger out of me that I didn't know was lurking in the corners. I took a deep inhale and tried to calm myself down. *This is going to be a good trip. It's okay if my memory is still not fully there. I've accomplished so much!* I thought.

But a nagging feeling lingered that I might not be able to connect with Carl's family and friends because I was still a little off. However, I wiped the worries away and focused on our upcoming trip. My mind wandered to all the possibilities of new adventures that we would have. Although, the closer we got to Minneapolis, the more my nerves were on end. It was hard for me to keep calm as we pulled up to the airport. Plus, my head felt like it was thrumming as though it was a drum from the ride.

I gave Mavry a tight squeeze and thanked her while I watched her bright red hair bounce back into her old wagon and drive away. As soon as she was in the distance, I was relieved that I didn't need to hide my pain anymore. Carl could already tell just by looking at me that I wasn't feeling the best. So, he took my backpack and carried it while he had his backpack on his back.

Once we got inside the airport, something weighed on me and I needed to rest. We had time to spare. After we checked in, we found a place near where I could rest a little while we figured out which gate. I kept taking deep breaths, holding, and then breathing out deeply. My thoughts strayed. But I kept bringing them back to focus on feeling better. Carl disappeared while I worked on myself, and he quickly came back with an orange juice. "Here, drink up. This should help you feel better." He said as he handed the juice to me carefully.

My heart began to feel warm, and I could feel tears starting to form in my eyes. But I pushed the tears away and said, "Thank you! You seem to always know what I need." He smirked at me and teased me by saying, "Well, you trained me well!" I chuckled and he smiled at me cheekily. After gulping down the juice, I started feeling much better. The pounding lessened and I was able to think again. The two of us started heading towards our gate.

Once we were on the airplane, my heart hammered away as I sat in my chair. This was the first flight that I had done since my accident. So, I quickly found out that my head was having a bit of trouble dealing with the pressure. I coaxed it to calm down and eventually, was able to sleep for an hour or two. After about 12 hours, we made it to Reykjavik, Iceland, and since we only had our backpacks, we didn't have to wait for luggage. However, we arrived there late at night and our next flight was the next day in the evening. So, Carl and I snuggled up on the hard floor of the airport and slept. It was a good thing that we had our sleeping bags since it was a little breezy there.

After about 5 hours of sleeping, a loud buzzing from a vacuum woke us up. It was about 6 am and time for us to start moving. Still with sleep in our eyes, we both rolled up our sleeping bags and headed to the bathrooms to do morning routines. After that, both of us agreed that tea was needed. So, we got some before we headed out to explore the city since we had a whole day there. The air was fresh, and it didn't feel like the cities that I was used to. There was a lot of land but not so much for buildings. We walked all over and ended up lying in some grass in a park for a bit.

Now, exhausted as can be but exhilarated from all the new experiences, we hopped on the last flight to our destination, Stockholm, Sweden. I don't know what I was expecting. But I didn't think that Sweden would have so many forests scattered over the country. Once I got out of the airport and breathed in the fresh air, my nerves finally relaxed. Carl led the way since he knew where we were going. When he was younger, he used to go to a circus school in Stockholm. So, he still had some friends around.

As we wandered further away from the airport, I noticed the Swedish signs and my confidence dropped. In that same instant, I started seeing the English signs and my fears withered away. Their language here is

Swedish. However, about 90% percent of Swedes are fluent in English, which makes it easier for tourists. A huge relief overtook me since I would be able to talk with his family and friends with no issues.

While we walked down the streets, I could overhear people talking. Their voices went up and down as though they were talking in a melody. I wasn't used to hearing Swedish and hadn't heard Carl speak in it much since he'd been in the USA. But as I listened, it just reaffirmed to me that we were in another country where life is lived differently than what I'm used to. Excitement stirred within me with a mix of anxiousness. But I reminded myself that *everything will work out, it always does. Plus, I'm with Carl, who invited me here.* I thought this as I waved those uncertain feelings away.

The city was so full of life and everyone we met had a huge smile on their face. *So, this is Sweden.* I thought as I reveled in the joy surrounding me. For being a city, Stockholm has a lot of nature spread throughout. There's an abundance of crystal-clear water as well since Stockholm is made up of fourteen islands. Once we dropped off our bags at one of Carl's friend's places, he stared at me with a twinkle in his eye. All I could think of was, *what did I do?* He quickly grabbed my hand and told his friend that we would meet up later and we scurried out the door.

"What's going on?" I asked him quizzically as he

dropped my hand. A huge smile crept onto his face, and he said, "I have something that I want to show you." It took us about 20–30 minutes until we made it to the building that he wanted to show me and once we got inside, my jaw dropped. Every direction I looked there were books covering all the walls. The building was a circle, and it wrapped in such a way that it looked surreal. My heart leapt for joy!

A way to my heart is through books. Libraries and bookstores are my hidden guilty pleasures. I could be lost here for hours. However, I don't think that my head would have let that happen. As I stared at it all in amazement, I felt like I was a kid again. All I could say to him was, "Wow!" Then I quickly took off up the stairs to start exploring and looking at the books, taking in everything with all my senses. The smells of the books, the touch of the grainy papers and hard covers, the sounds of people in silence turning pages and the fresh water from the drinking fountain.

After a bit of time, I started to feel guilty with staying there so long. Plus, my body was losing its buzz from the newfound gem. It was time to check out another great place, Gamla Stan, Old Town. When we walked around this area of Stockholm, it felt like I was teleported to another time with cobblestone roads and stone buildings with overgrown trees near them. Even though it had the feeling of being old, I could sense that it had many tranquil spots. My head began hammering from all the new stimulations and Carl could sense it. So, he brought me to a cozy little cafe where we could sit outside and enjoy the calm breeze near a huge tree sprawled out. This branched out over this open area which was surrounded by all the tall buildings.

It felt nice to sit down and relax after walking and exploring for hours. My body was sore, and I knew this was just the beginning of our day here. Besides that, it was Midsommar, meaning we would be celebrating it with his Swedish friends. A fear started to bubble within me. But I gulped that down and worked on being in the present moment. I took in a deep breath and looked at the gigantic tree in amazement as I held onto my piping hot teacup. Suddenly, I could feel someone staring at me and I abruptly met Carl's eyes. His gaze averted mine and my heart began to patter as I avoided making eye contact again.

Even now, I sometimes forget that we are together and that we are married. When that popped up in my mind, a whirlwind of feelings came alive. I began feeling my heartbeat racing and butterflies in my stomach. *Why am I acting like a girl with a crush?!* I thought as my face began to heat up. After a few minutes of silence, we both came out of our fogs and went back to normal. He told me more about Old Town while I stared in fascination as we walked to meet up with Carl's old friends.

In that group, there was a girl with long dark

straight hair that Carl had a fling with and when she found out that we were married, she couldn't take her chocolate eyes off me. Jealousy emitted from her as she stared at me with daggers in her eyes. *Woah… She needs to chill.* I thought as I tried to dodge her gaze by talking to one of Carl's other friends. *There's no need for adding more heat to her already hateful glances.* So, I disregarded that feeling I was getting from her and ended up turning my back towards her.

We walked as a group to one of the parks and as we got closer, a liveliness filled the air. Midsommar was happening and this was the time of the year when the sun was up nearly all day. There were 1,000s of people spread across the park dressed in different colorful hues and carrying baskets for fika. A huge maypole stood tall that was covered in a variety of flowers with brightly colored ribbons wrapped around it. This happened from when people had danced around it. While we walked closer, I could feel the wind beat along with the music. This feeling went throughout my body and filled me with such happiness. *Wow! So, this is Midsommar. How magical!* I thought as we strolled further into the crowd of people.

The cool wind whipped through the open area, making it pleasant in the warm sunshine. Every direction that I looked, I could see smiling faces or hear laughs in the distance. Everyone was having a great time and booze was in abundance scattered on picnic blankets and in coolers. Besides that, there were chairs spread out and the music pulsated in the breeze. Midsommar is a time to celebrate the longest day of the year. It's the summer solstice and the time when life comes to nature. As I thought that, I noticed all the blooming flowers in the flower beds and some of the trees with blooms sprinkled on them.

From that spot, I could see the speakers in the distance and the stage booming with life. We didn't need to be close to feel the power from the sound. It echoed in the wind and made my whole-body shake. This was intense yet welcoming since the feeling was full of joy. Plus, it was great being surrounded by so much stimulation and it all being entertaining! That's pretty unusual for me to have fun around such a big group. I had been avoiding big crowds since my accident. But being engulfed in this feeling, I didn't want to run, I wanted to be immersed as much as I could. Suddenly, I came back from my thoughts and took in my surroundings in a new light.

My heart skipped a beat as I stared back at the group of people and seeing Carl's smile left me breathless. It must be nice for him to be comfortable and speak with old friends in his native tongue again. *I wonder if he missed it.* I thought. Then sadness overtook me because I thought of myself being the reason that he gave up his happiness. But quickly reality came back as his friend Jonathon started to talk to me as he nudged me with his elbow playfully. His goatee and shaggy blonde hair added to his charm. Jonathan's skinny muscular body was in great shape since he used to go to circus school with Carl.

But nowadays, he takes to the floor, dances, and plays music for all kinds of audiences. When I listened to him sing, I felt like he was telling my story along with all kinds of others that I've heard. The passion behind the songs would teleport me and bring me to where I could walk in the steps of the stories he was singing about. I felt ecstatic when I got to hang out with him since he's such a talented guy and easy to get along with. "Helloo!? Bonnie?" He said as he waved his hand in front of my face. "Ohh, sorry." I stammered as I began to blush. I had lost my reality again and now he had found out that I dazed out.

A stabbing pain of a possible rejection dived deep down inside of me. As I held my breath waiting for him to change his attitude, he didn't. It didn't bother him at all that I went into a trance, and I felt like a weight was taken off my shoulders. He started asking me, "So, what do ya think of Midsommar, and what about Stockholm?"

"It's amazing! I can feel all the love and how happy people are. This must be a time that everyone looks forward to." I said gleefully as my eyes lit up.

He chuckled and said, "Yup! That's why we endure the winter!"

After a fun couple of days relishing in the festivities, it was time to head to Carl's parents' home in Sunne, Sweden. The ride on the train was smooth and swift since we were on the fast train. Plus, the views were magical as we went further into the forests. I could see the lakes in the distance sparkling with life. It felt so peaceful, and I had this feeling of serenity wash over me. In about two hours or so, we were in Karlstad, the big city of the county, which is only around an hour away from Sunne.

Out of nowhere my head was starting to feel every movement. But I reminded myself that we were almost there. Carl gave me a tight squeeze on my shoulders and pointed out the window. I followed his finger, and the view was unforgettable. All the pains in my head were forgotten as I took in the deep blue pools of water and the bright green pine and birch trees. The nature outside the train looked mystical and reminded me of a fairy tale. I could imagine another kind of way of living with magical beings frolicking in the fields and living in the forests.

As I thought about this, Carl began telling me stories about trolls, fairies, and witches. Many Swedes believe these things to be true. As though these things are just a part of our world. No questions or anything. A curiosity inched through me, and I wanted to know more about all the tales. So, I kept pestering Carl to get more out of him, but he left it at that.

This land became even more interesting to me, and

I stared in awe out the window. Finally, we made it to his parents, and their house was surrounded by the wilderness. It felt fully isolated from the outer world. Besides that, it's a little oasis from the small town where we could fully connect with nature.

Since being in Sweden, I quickly noticed that they have loads of red houses. So, when we got to Carl's parents, it was nice to see a color out of the norm. Their house had a black tinge on the wooden walls. Not too far from their house was an old tiny red outhouse. This property had a few buildings that showed how much time, and effort had been put into the place along with all the tools they had for future projects. Besides having their house, they have a small cabin next to it that they had as their original home. But over the years, they needed to expand since they had 3 boys and thus, this little cabin turned into a great spot for the boys as their homebase once they got older.

My head was thankful for all the scenery, and I sat outside, enjoying the breeze and soaking up the sun. At that moment, my head eased, and I could think a lot more clearly. His mom, Suzanne, talked with me and asked how everything was going. I glanced at her, trying to hold back the pain and I told her, "I'm slowly adjusting to the time difference and the sun." She chuckled at that. She knew that the sun could be something to get used to since it stays in the sky for most of the day during this time of the year.

Carl started talking with his mom and I was swept back within myself. Everything felt right when I was in nature. I felt closer to my roots, and this relaxed me. As I sat there with my eyes closed, I imagined my life here and how much of a blessing it would be to be surrounded by the outdoors regularly. That thought alone brought joy to me and at that moment a bird's melody echoed in the breeze. My eyes fluttered open and I took a deep inhale. It felt like everything was lining up correctly and I felt a calling to stay here.

After the two weeks were up, it was time to head back and at that moment I realized that I could see myself living here. My mind drifted back to reality, and I held Carl's hand with such love and appreciation for him. I'm so thankful that he's in my life. I could feel the tears start to well in my eyes. But I didn't give in. He doesn't need to know. He already knows so much about my weaknesses already. I wouldn't give him another!

CHAPTER 11

Moving to a New Country (Present)

Once we discussed the details and I researched more about Sweden, I was set on moving there. So, in the summertime, our furry family, Carl and I said our goodbyes and had all our stuff boxed and were transported into cars that were going to Sweden. This was a big step for me, moving to another country. I felt nervous yet excited all balled up in one. But, overall, it felt like this was right. My head was still not back to normal. However, I had time to work on myself while we were helping my family's business. My ego was back, and I had overcome the first hurdles in getting better. Even so, I had a lot more to go. But I felt at ease as thoughts flowed out about how lost I had felt. However now, I can do so much! There is so much that I have accomplished!

We had been in the USA for around three or so years. As I thought about how Carl had got up and moved to be with me in another country, it seemed silly if I couldn't do the same. *If it doesn't work, then we can move back or find a new home somewhere else.* I thought as I swallowed my fears. That's when I took the ultimate step, and I haven't looked back!

While we were working on settling in a small cabin with an outhouse out in the middle of the woods in

Sweden, the feeling of being surrounded by the wilderness called to me. Since we lived right in it, I could feel strings come out of me and connect with the environment. I felt like I was where I was meant to be. The birds chirped cheerfully as they flew by, and our cats meowed as they scampered on their own adventures outside. During this time, Clyde was most happy by my side, no matter what. So, when we went on our forest walk, he and the cats were bouncing around through the deep woody area.

The light wind was soothing, and I could feel the trees murmuring. Once we walked in, my head felt lighter. It was as though this was what I needed to help heal. No matter how many times I wandered down this trail, I was blown away by its beauty. The moss covered the ground, and it felt cooler with the trees covering the sky above. As I strolled further in, I could hear the small stream flowing, which added to the wilderness. Birds chirped wildly and flew out of the vegetation as we got closer.

With every step, the crunch of leaves and twigs seemed to echo in the vast opening. My mind was beginning to clear, and I felt at peace. Every direction that I looked there was life. This took away any stressful thoughts that I had. *I've found my home.* I thought gleefully as I spun with my arms out and laughed. Clyde joyfully ran around me and did a happy bark while the cats stared at us from a distance. My heart was racing, and I felt the urge to push on. The atmosphere engulfed me and my whole body felt like this was right. Since moving to Sweden, I've felt better day by day. However, I would still have bad days where my head would act like it wasn't screwed on tight enough.

My hubby, Carl has always been a handyman and when we came back here, he would work in the forest cutting down trees. Well, one of those days while he had his headphones on, blazing music, I was inside doing dishes. Days before, I had painted the cupboards and the cabinets to bring a little color to the kitchen. So, I kept myself busy and I felt useful that I could, even with my head pains that would come randomly. At this moment, I was so concentrated on putting the dishes away that I wasn't fully aware of the upper cabinet that I had left open. As I stood up, I hit it perfectly with my head. Immediately, I felt woozy and had trouble focusing.

My world began to swirl, and I quickly grabbed the countertop. A deep breath escaped me and then I touched my head. From that, I could feel a warm wet liquid and as I pulled my hand away, I looked at it in disbelief. My head was bleeding, and it wasn't just a little. It was dripping down from my head. In an instant, it was on my jean shorts and a little on my grey tank top. I was consumed in guilt as I realized what I had done to myself.

How could I let this happen? Come on, I'm better than this. I thought as I treaded slowly on the walk of shame to Carl in the woods. Once I got to the road, I saw him not too far away. It didn't take long before he took one look at me and his jaw dropped. One look at me screamed that I stepped out of a horror film. A streak of blood dripped down my face onto my tank top and I held out my hands so that I couldn't get covered in it any more than I already was. Carl urgently turned off his roaring chainsaw, put it down, took off his headphones, and rushed towards me.

"What happened!?" He yelled as he got closer to me. I stared at him sheepishly. I felt like an idiot. As he got closer, I explained what had happened. After that, he looked at the point where I was bleeding from, and he saw that I made a little puncture. I must have hit the corner of the cabinet door just perfectly. So, he ushered me back to the cabin, helped wash me up and bandaged me. Since I needed help, I felt like a kid that needed a parent… I was immersed in shame.

My thoughts swirled, *aren't I good enough to take care of myself? I guess not.* In that moment, a feeling of defeat overtook me. He could tell that I was beating myself up, so he said to me, "Why don't we watch a movie? I can make popcorn." Once he said that, a smile inched onto my face. I began to salivate as I imagined the yummy warm salty puffs going into my mouth. I love popcorn and his homemade popcorn is the best!

After I switched into my pajamas, we cuddled up in the bed and started watching a show while we munched on the delicious popcorn. These moments would engulf me in peace.

The solitude living in the forest away from anyone at first was nice and calming. But then it started to weigh on me. I had no friends and knew no one except Carl, his friends and family. So, I was starting to feel more alone than what was anticipated and since my head was foggy at times, I felt helpless. There were still days when I was stuck in bed because the weather banged on my head. Other times, I just wanted someone to talk to that was a friend. However, Carl and I had one car, and he used it for work. So, there would be many lonely nights since he worked on trains and would have to sleep away. During this time, I would keep myself busy by going on walks and studying Swedish. Besides that, I started working on my travel blog a lot more consistently.

Something that I still did was drift in and out of myself. At times, this would be great to help my inner workings. But other times, my ego wouldn't be on my side and would point out how alone I was. Tears would stroll down my cheeks, and I thought about how comforting it had been to have some friends around. Right then, I switched my thoughts from sadness to thankfulness and then I started to feel better. After that, Carl and I had talked about getting another car so that

I could go into town whenever. We quickly found a great used one that helped me spread my wings.

Sweden gives a great opportunity to the foreigners of all ages by helping them learn Swedish for free. When I found out about this, excitement brimmed within me. I would be able to understand more and be able to talk with Carl in his first language. Besides that, I would meet more people. My heart sped up as I thought of all the new adventures that we could have with me being able to understand the language. Being a part of the conversations with his family and friends would make me feel like I was more included. There wouldn't be a language barrier anymore.

My heart skipped a beat when I came to the classroom door. I was excited to meet new friends, and this was just the beginning! I've always been a friendly outgoing person. So, I didn't care about people's past or where they were from. I know that a person is a person. Once I started going to SFI to learn Swedish, I quickly made friends. My heart hammered to life because I thrive being around others.

So, I took my first step in the door and a wave of voices in Arabic and in Dutch surrounded me. I was taken aback. I don't know what kind of languages I was expecting to hear. But it was interesting! I started to feel like a curious child because I wanted to get to know as many of the people as I could. Languages have always fascinated me along with cultures. So, I saw this opportunity as a gold mine of knowledge!

Now, it was the thought of bringing different cultures together that led me to create the Kultural Fest. This was an event with music, workshops, and booths. Each booth represented a different country since this small town had people from all over. These booths showed off their culture with traditional foods, and little trinkets or whatever the person wanted to show representing their country. For the USA, I had my homemade album that was photos from Carl and my honeymoon trip. From this, I wanted people to see the different places in the USA. All my thoughts swarmed around American food as being fast food. So, I finally decided to make deviled eggs instead. It was a common food in my family.

The sun heated the area, and a cool breeze added to it being a great day for the event. The grassy areas were welcoming, and the river nearby added to the peaceful atmosphere. Besides having the tables spread out, we had a tent put up for the kiddos and I did duck, duck, goose with them for a bit. Along with that, some kids had the chance to transform into tigers or puppies with face paint! Another fun activity was macramé for anyone that was interested in learning. My friend had loads of people surrounding her as she showed them how to tie the strings properly to make the bracelets. On top of this, there was live music that reverberated in the wind. We had over 400 people come, and I was astounded! I was able to do this even with a brain injury and being in a new country! Now, I have proven that following your heart is the way to go.

Among everything I was doing, I know that nature helped me with healing tremendously. Being encircled by it would make me feel at ease and all my worries would be swept away as I basked in the wilderness on a walk or savored just being in it. The more I followed my heart, the more my head felt better. So, I kept pushing forward, going on walks, and reflecting on the good things in my life. That gave me the drive to progress further.

I just had issues with my head at least once a month when I couldn't even leave my bed. But it was getting better and soon it became a lot less. My heart felt at peace in our home out in the forest. Having nature so close felt right. So, my life, I still had some healing to do. But I was feeling happy and that this was where I was meant to be.

CHAPTER 12

Your Mindset Holds Power

My past felt like a whirlwind of ups and downs. I had a lot of healing to do. Plus, there were many things that I couldn't do because of my head. From that, my mind was opened and it made me realize more about life. There's so much that we take for granted. It isn't until it's out of our reach, that we seem to want it the most. My traumatic brain injury made this obvious to me. There were days when I had to accept that I wouldn't be the same in my brain and sometimes it was hard to get over. But from the years of healing, I've learned that we are always changing, it's part of life and this is just a new journey for me.

Besides that, I've found that finding your passion is what pushes us forward. Without it, we are stuck in limbo, a mucky place that feels wrong in every way. Maybe you don't feel happy nor sad. But a feeling of 'bleh' is not a way to live. So, find what drives you forward and hold on to it tightly. Wherever you have passion is where you should be.

Before my car accident, I never noticed the impact that we get from being around others. This was painfully known after my car crash though. From just being around a big group of people, I would get a piercing pain in my head. I even had trouble going to stores for a while there. As I walked into the store, my body would cringe, and my head would throb as I became overstimulated with all the lights, sounds, and people. My stomach would churn, and I would feel sick. So, our store trips would usually be around 10–20 minutes. Once we got home, I would feel exhausted and have to relax for the rest of the day.

Another thing to note is the power that nature and the weather had on my healing process. When we ventured to Florida during the winter months, I remember that many of the days I would be stuck in my parents' RV. Every move that I would make came with a roaring pain in my head. The humidity and I weren't friends. So, at times it felt like a tug of war, and I was losing! Days turned into weeks, then into months. Most of our time in Florida ended up with me inside reading while everyone else would get to explore.

At this time, I would be wallowing in my own pity since they could play outside, and I was stuck on the couch. However, I worked on thinking about how lucky I was. Joy overflowed in my heart as memories flooded in my mind about being able to come to Florida and be with my parents, our furry family, and Carl. When I switched my thinking, a wave of calmness would take over. But this wasn't something I could easily change. Some days were better than others. Besides that, this time in my life involved a lot of depression, anxiety, and frustration.

Along my healing journey, the outdoors played a huge role. It was a way that I was able to connect with my inner self even more. Not only that, but it also helped me become grounded. So, each time that I went out into the wilderness, a relaxing feeling would take hold of me. My stress and any bad feelings would disappear, leaving me to reflect inward and focus more on what needed my attention. For instance, when we hiked up Yosemite National Park, I could hear my inner voice a lot clearer, and what I had to do for myself. I felt the pull, the urge to push forward, and doing this showed my mind and body that I was serious about healing.

On our road trip in the USA, it was the wilderness that whispered to me once again. I felt in harmony when we would visit a national park, or anytime we ventured outside. The air that I breathed in worked its magic on my body and when I was being active with walking, hiking, or yoga, my body praised me. Once I did this, it gave off a feeling of accomplishment, as though it was giving me all the right signs that I was going in the right direction. At this moment, my mind would clear, and I felt connected with myself.

During this time, I also realized how important gratitude was and staying positive even when it felt like it was the end. There's always good in every situation. You just have to be patient and find it. Along with our road trip was a feeling of chaos and emotions whirling within me. It was my first year of healing and I was recently married. First off, I was used to single life and having that freedom. Now I had someone else on my radar and it felt strange. But he let me feel as free as I needed to and he understood that if he didn't, I would feel like a caged bird.

We definitely hit some rough spots as we traveled together. But we endured and both of us grew from it. Even though my healing journey was a solo battle, he was there. He may not have fully understood what was happening in my mind. However, he let me know that if I needed anything, he was there. *What more could I ask for?* I thought as I realized just how blessed I was to have my best friend by my side on the toughest journey of my life.

I never knew how scary and sad it can be to face yourself from within. Although the more I did that, the less scary it felt and the more that I accepted myself. We, as humans tend to avoid coming into contact with ourselves. All of us have some baggage that we've packed far far away in our closet that we never want it to see light. But avoiding the issue(s) within doesn't get rid of the problem. In actuality, it creates more problems that can come to the surface and give us physical issues.

After the first two years of healing, I began to feel more like myself. My ego had come back as a newer, better version, and it felt like I belonged in my body. I still had a long way to go though, and it wasn't until about 7 years before I felt as healed as I would be. At that time, my hubby and I had finally decided to bring a new life to our family, and I gave my birthday to our little boy. We share the same birthday and what a great gift to be given!

Now, becoming a mom was a hard decision to make. Memories of the past pain that I have had in my head and how there were days when I couldn't leave the bed from it would come. So, I thought that I would be a horrible mom, not able to function well enough to take care of a little one. But once we finally agreed on having a baby, that feeling of insecurity was lifted and our bundle of joy came. Since then, I'm grateful that I didn't let my fear override my life.

Ten years later, the pain has softened, and it has become almost nonexistent. I can be around groups of people again without pain since I've learned to manage my inner self. With my inner healing, my eyes have been opened. Now this is an ongoing process.

When I'm in nature, I feel more in tune with myself. Something that I reflected on while in the outdoors was that when I was younger, it felt like I needed some kind of validation. As if I could only get that from being surrounded by people. Nowadays that's not needed. I can have days by myself and feel completely happy.

Through this whole healing journey, I've learned just how important the environment is for us physically and mentally. Besides that, there are other modalities that have helped me through the tough times. For instance, my go-to while I was healing subconsciously was meditation. I did it whenever I zoned out and it wasn't until I wrote this that I realized that's what I was doing all those times. Another thing that helped me was yoga, getting my body to move and stretch helped me a ton. Plus, it gave me the courage to see what I could and couldn't do with my body without being completely damaging. I didn't let my traumatic brain injury limit me. Instead, I used it more as a new way to understand myself and something to grow from.

These past couple of years I've also learned the importance of a good mindset and how to retrain your subconscious. It's been an interesting time, but I've been feeling even more alive than I have in the past. From that, I've been opening doors that I never even knew that I had. Now, a great tip I learned is that we get to choose the life we have, and everything always happens for a reason. For me, regarding my TBI, that was what I needed so I would slow down. I wasn't listening any other way, so a few intense hits on the head were needed!

So, some great tips on healing yourself would be meditation, affirmation, yoga, a visualization journal, and a gratitude list. These are some things that I've formed into a daily habit that have made a whole world of a difference. I start my day off with yoga in the morning. Then, I do a daily walk in the surrounding forests and while I lavish in the light breeze, I visualize my life as I want it to be. With every step I take, I imagine that my feet are tree roots that are going into the ground, holding onto the earth's core. From this, I take unconditional love and bring it back into me. This fills me with love and joy. Once I've completed my walk, I then go into the bathroom and say affirmations to myself as I look in a mirror. This tends to get me pumped up for the rest of the day!

As I go through my day, I stay in a positive mindset and let any bad stuff roll off me. Once it gets later in the day, it's time for my nightly routine and this involves my visualization journal. As I put the pen to the paper, I imagine my dreams flowing through me. As though they are happening in the present moment. I use all the senses, and I bring out the feelings that I would have in what I'm writing about. While writing, it's like I've been teleported through each word and into my writing.

After doing that, it's time for my gratitude list, which is at least 10 items. Every sentence that I write down is filled with gratitude. In that moment, I would have to feel it in order to give it any power. Finally, my day ends with me meditating right before going to bed. I focus on my breathing and my future as if it is already here. Besides that, I fully listen to my body and to what it's trying to tell me.

Time and time again I'm still learning. But I can help guide many from my own experiences. We can say that I was the guinea pig in the process, and you are the prodigy of all the work that I've learned. All that I've gained knowledge on is what we need to do on ourselves to become the better version of ourselves. It feels great when you can understand yourself. One of the best ways is to realize that the things in life that make you satisfied aren't on the outside but on the inside.

After 10 years, I've experienced that we truly never stop learning, and working on ourselves is an ongoing process. You can't expect to do all the work and then just stop. That's not how it works. We, as people, tend to want the easy route. But if you truly want to get better, it takes effort and time.

Thank you for reading my book and please share my book with all that you know to help inspire even more people. Or you can book a time with me so that you have some guidance on how you can take on your own obstacles. Life can get tough. So, it helps when you have support, and I'd love to help guide you in the right direction. If you would like to hear more about my story, then check out any of my webinars, podcasts that I've been on, or any of my speaking engagements.

misfitwanders.com

About the Author

Dani Rosenblad James wants to inspire individuals to overcome life's obstacles and take on the transformative power of resilience. With a deep appreciation for the importance of nature, Dani seeks to connect people to the wonders of the natural world and highlight the critical role it plays in our lives.

Through her own journey of overcoming challenges, including a traumatic brain injury, Dani discovered the healing and rejuvenating effects of nature and the power within us. She harnesses this knowledge to advocate for sustainable travel practices along with helping guide people to learn how to connect the mind with the body.

As the driving force behind Misfit Wanders, Dani shares her passion for eco-conscious travel, intertwining together captivating stories of nature's marvels and diverse cultures. Through her blog, speaking engagements, and one-on-one coaching, she empowers others to take on meaningful journeys that honor both the planet and personal growth.

She's written for H.A.N.N.A Magazine, Force Magazine, Becoming an Unstoppable Woman Magazine, Road.Travel, GoNomad, Inspiring Lives Magazine, and Full Suitcase. Besides her busy work life, she has a son, a husband and lives in Sweden. Find more about her at misfitwanders.com.